I Love My Dog

embroidery

380 Stitch Motifs for Dog Moms and Dads

MakikoArt

Design & Stitching: MakikoArt (Oksana Kokovkina)

Embroidered Motifs for Dog Lovers!

I Love My Dog Embroidery is a celebration of man's best friend with more than 380 adorable embroidery motifs showing dogs and puppies in action. Stitch a wide array of active canines: catching frisbees, rolling on their backs; celebrating holidays; sitting in teacups; smelling flowers; being angels; and just being their completely lovable selves. You can even choose from one of your favorite breeds, whether it's a Labrador Retriever, Siberian Husky, Boston Terrier, or French Bulldog. Also included are project inspirations that show ideas for adding your stitched motifs to pencil cases, handkerchiefs, wearable apparel, and other fun gifts.

In addition to motifs, projects, and instructions by popular, professional embroidery artist MakikoArt (Oksana Kokovkina), motifs have been designed and stitched by a talented team of professional embroiderers: Mia Alexi of How Could You? Clothing; Elizabeth Dabczynski of Stitch People; Anja Lehmann of Solipandi; Valentina Castillo Mora of Insanitynice; Chloe Redfern of Chloe Redfern Embroidery; and Miho Starling of mipomipo handmade.

Fifteen basic stitches are used to create all the motifs in the book. Instructions for how to embroider them will inspire beginners and refresh those with more advanced skills. Each finished design is shown fully stitched with a photograph, along with instructions on how to recreate them yourself, and templates you can use to transfer the designs to your chosen fabric. With designs from very simple outlines to more intricate, multi-colored motifs, there really is something here for every level of stitcher.

I Love My Dog Embroidery contains so many adorable ideas for embroidering your furry friends, you'll never find yourself in the doghouse (unless you want to stitch one!).

— The Editors

Designs, Project Inspiration, and Instructions

MakikoArt / Oksana Kokovkina
See pages 18–27 and 38–55
makiko.at
instagram.com/makikoart

Plus Designs by These Contributing Artists

Insanitynice / Valentina Castillo Mora
See pages 6–13
instagram.com/insanitynice

Chloe Redfern Embroidery / Chloe Redfern
See pages 14 & 15
chloeredfern.co.uk

Solipandi / Anja Lehmann
See pages 16 & 17
solipandi.com

How Could You? Clothing / Mia Alexi
See pages 28–31
howcouldyouclothing.com

Stitch People / Elizabeth Dabczynski
See pages 32–35
stitchpeople.com

Miho Starling / mipomipo handmade
See pages 36 & 37
mipomipohandmade.etsy.com

Contents

All-Time Favorites

Stitch Guides & Templates: Pages 56–59
Design & Stitching: Insanitynice (Valentina Castillo Mora)

13 Labrador Retriever
14 German Shepherd
15 Golden Retriever
16 English Bulldog
17 Beagle
18 Poodle
19 Rottweiler
20 Yorkshire Terrier
21 Boxer
22 German Short-Haired Pointer
23 Siberian Husky
24 Dachshund

Little Friends

Stitch Guides & Templates: Pages 60-63
Design & Stitching: Insanitynice (Valentina Castillo Mora)

37 French Bulldog
38 Cavalier King Charles Spaniel
39 Corgi
40 Shih Tzu
41 Chihuahua
42 Bichon Frise
43 Jack Russell Terrier
44 West Highland White Terrier
45 Boston Terrier
46 Maltese
47 Pomeranian
48 Pug

Big Friends

Stitch Guides & Templates: Pages 64-67
Design & Stitching: Insanitynice (Valentina Castillo Mora)

61 Great Dane
62 Doberman Pinscher
63 Bernese Mountain Dog
64 Newfoundland
65 Akita
66 English Mastiff
67 Rhodesian Ridgeback
68 Belgian Malinois
69 St. Bernard
70 Great Pyrenees
71 Bloodhound
72 Irish Wolfhound

More to Love

Stitch Guides & Templates: Pages 68–71
Design & Stitching: Insanitynice (Valentina Castillo Mora)

85 **American Pitbull Terrier**

86 **Basset Hound**

87 **Border Collie**

88 **Brittany Spaniel**

89 **English Cocker Spaniel**

90 **Standard Schnauzer**

91 **Chinese Shar-pei**

92 **Shetland Sheepdog**

93 **Shiba Inu**

94 **Soft-Coated Wheaten Terrier**

95 **Irish Setter**

96 **Weimaraner**

Just Call Me Spot

Stitch Guide & Template: Pages 72 & 73
Design & Stitching: Chloe Redfern Embroidery (Chloe Redfern)

Baby, I'm a Star!

Stitch Guide & Template: Pages 74 & 75

Design & Stitching: Chloe Redfern Embroidery (Chloe Redfern)

Won't You Be My Friend?

Stitch Guide & Template: Pages 76 & 77
Design & Stitching: Solipandi (Anja Lehmann)

Doggy Heaven

Stitch Guide & Template: Pages 78 & 79
Design & Stitching: Solipandi (Anja Lehmann)

I Love My Job

Stitch Guide & Template: Pages 80 & 81
Design & Stitching: MakikoArt (Oksana Kokovkina)

Sporty Pups

Stitch Guide & Template: Pages 82 & 83
Design & Stitching: MakikoArt (Oksana Kokovkina)

Getting Into Stuff

Stitch Guide & Template: Pages 84 & 85
Design & Stitching: MakikoArt (Oksana Kokovkina)

Getting Stuff Done

Stitch Guide & Template: Pages 86 & 87
Design & Stitching: MakikoArt (Oksana Kokovkina)

Dog Days

Stitch Guide & Template: Pages 88 & 89
Design & Stitching: MakikoArt (Oksana Kokovkina)

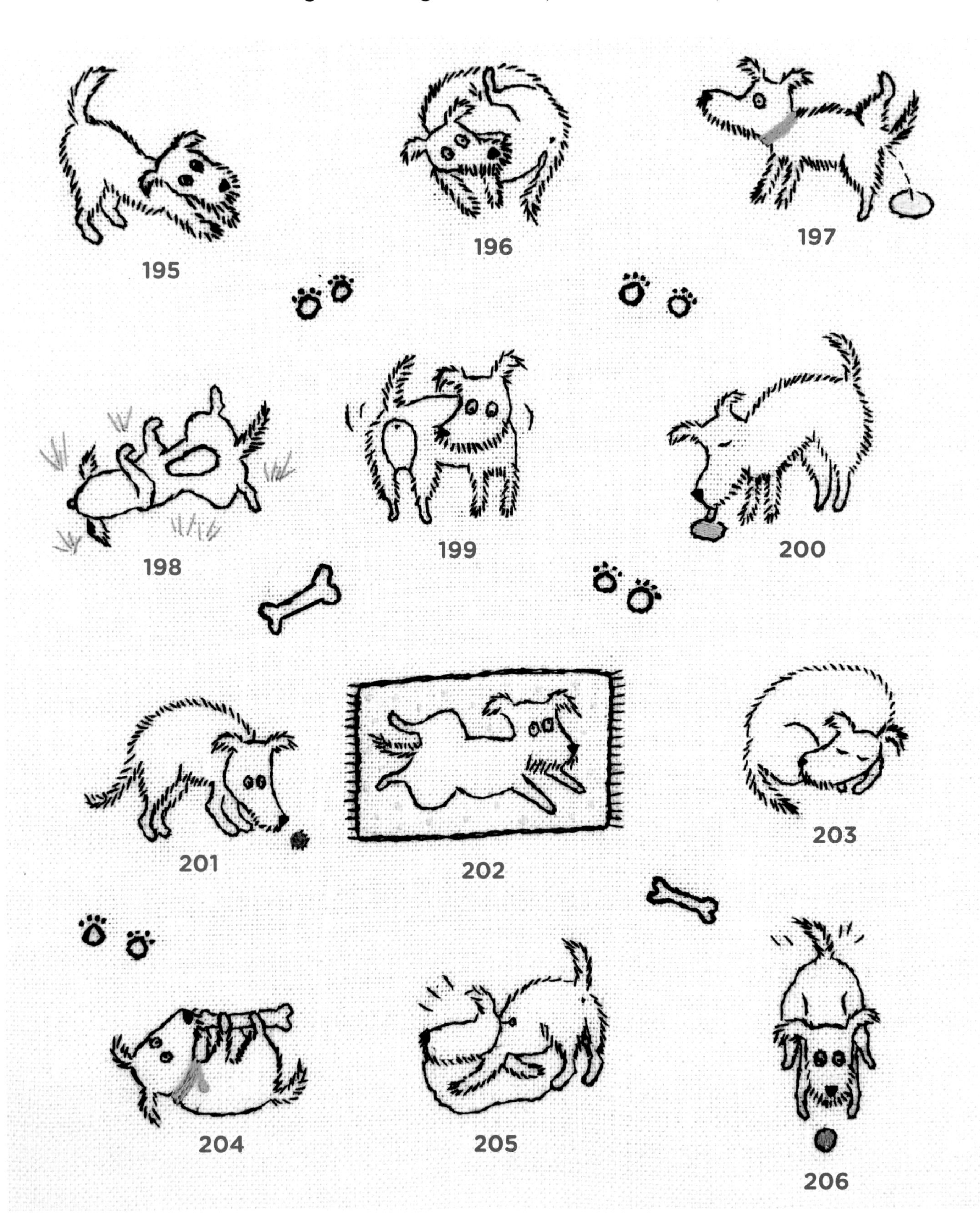

Scruffy Chic

Stitch Guide & Template: Pages 90 & 91
Design & Stitching: MakikoArt (Oksana Kokovkina)

Dazzling Dogs

Stitch Guide & Template: Pages 92 & 93
Design & Stitching: MakikoArt (Oksana Kokovkina)

Interspecies Love

Stitch Guide & Template: Pages 94 & 95
Design & Stitching: MakikoArt (Oksana Kokovkina)

Seasons & Celebrations

Stitch Guides & Templates: Pages 96–99
Design & Stitching: MakikoArt (Oksana Kokovkina)

253
254
255
256
257
258
259
260
261
262
263
264

Astrodogical Signs

Stitch Guides & Templates: Pages 100–103
Design & Stitching: How Could You? Clothing (Mia Alexi)

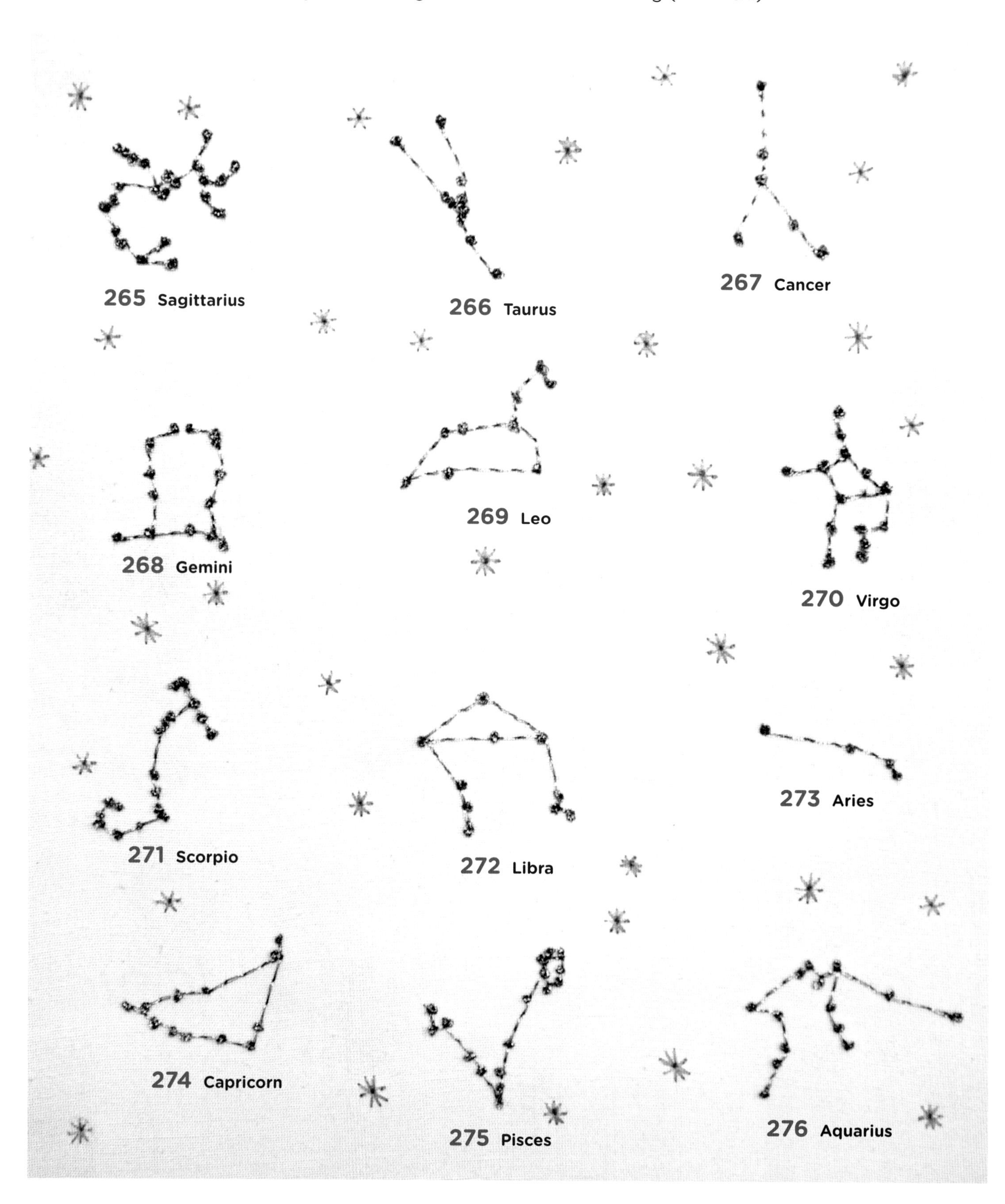

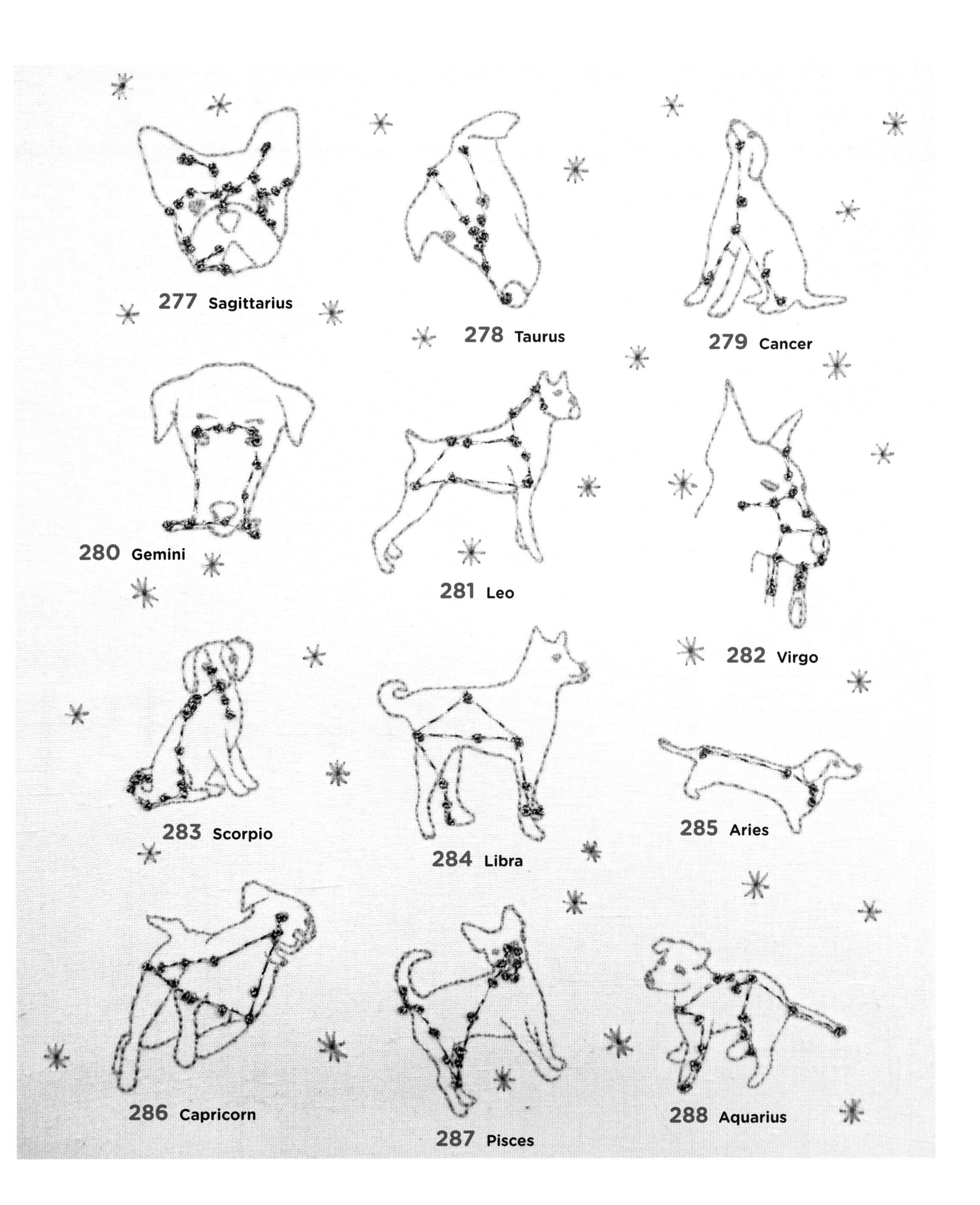
277 Sagittarius
278 Taurus
279 Cancer
280 Gemini
281 Leo
282 Virgo
283 Scorpio
284 Libra
285 Aries
286 Capricorn
287 Pisces
288 Aquarius

Alpha Dogs

Stitch Guides & Templates: Pages 104–107
Design & Stitching: How Could You? Clothing (Mia Alexi)

n
302
o
303
p
304
q
305
r
306
s
307
t
308
u
309
v
310
w
311
x
312
y
313
z
314

Look-Alikes: Pups & Their Peeps

Stitch Guides & Templates: Pages 108–111
Design & Stitching: Stitch People (Elizabeth Dabczynski)

315 border
316 human
317 dog

318 border
319 human
320 dog

321 border
322 human
323 dog

324 border
325 human
326 dog

327 border
328 human
329 dog

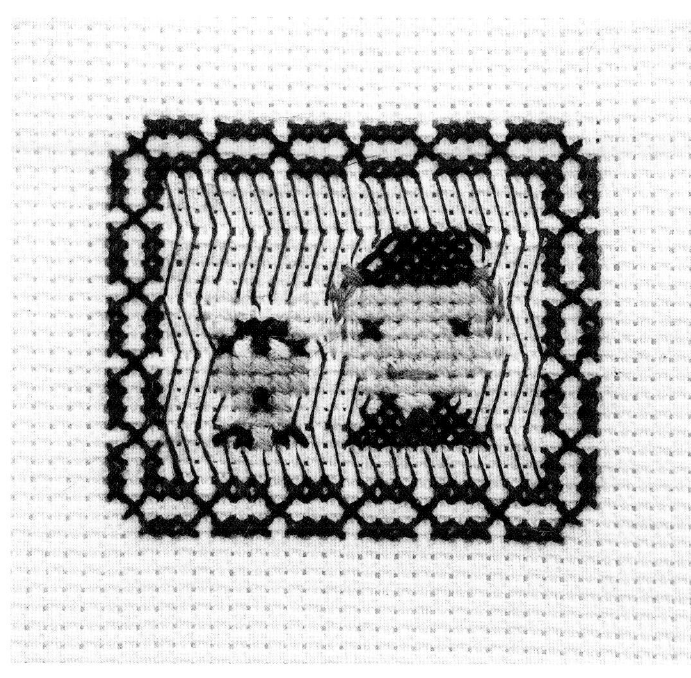

330 border
331 human
332 dog

333 border
334 human
335 dog

336 border
337 human
338 dog

Look-Alikes: Pups & Their Peeps

Stitch Guides & Templates: Pages 112–115
Design & Stitching: Stitch People (Elizabeth Dabczynski)

339 border
340 human
341 dog

342 border
343 human
344 dog

345 border
346 human
347 dog

348 border
349 human
350 dog

351 border
352 human
353 dog

354 border
355 human
356 dog

357 border
358 human
359 dog

360 border
361 human
362 dog

Me Time

Stitch Guide & Template: Pages 116 & 117
Design & Stitching: Miho Starling—mipomipo handmade

Doga Poses

Stitch Guide & Template: Pages 118 & 119
Design & Stitching: Miho Starling—mipomipo handmade

Project Inspirations

Design & Stitching: MakikoArt (Oksana Kokovkina)

The motifs in this book can be used to embellish a variety of fabrics and materials. Use these examples as a jumping-off point for creating your own unique projects and gifts.

Dog walking with style! Stitch your favorite motif on your dog's bandana.
Motif: Page 23.

Black-and-white puppy chic for your glasses case.
Motif: Page 23.

Stitch and frame a doggy motif that complements your decor.
Motif: Page 26.

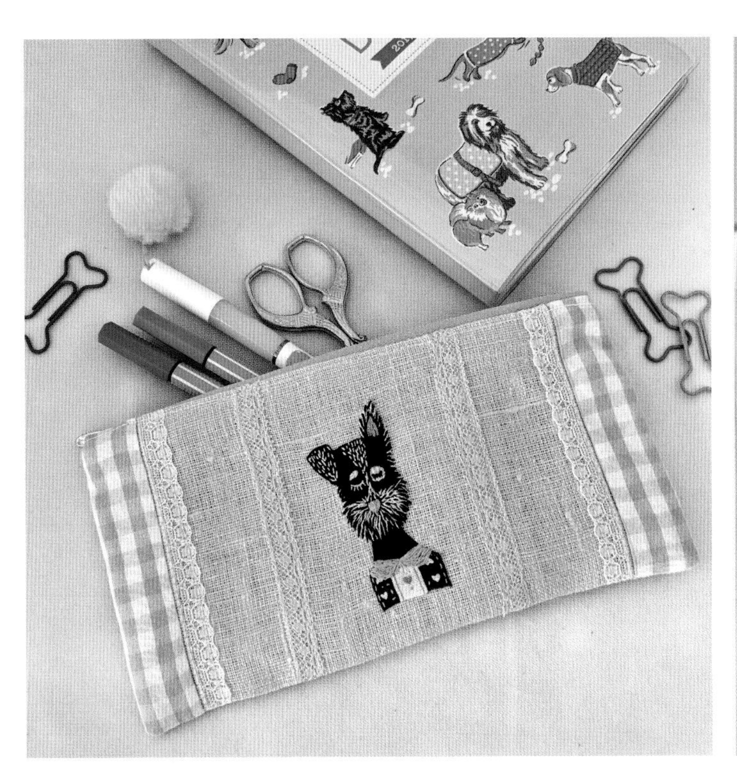

This adorable mutt looks right at home on a pencil case.
Motif: Page 23.

Load up this embroidered fanny pack with dog treats and take your pup a walk.
Motif: Page 19.

Stitch up a precious pooch and turn it into a pendant.
Motif: Page 27.

Embroider a design onto a denim shirt for a one-of-a-kind fashion statement.
Motif: Page 19.

Embroider one of the holiday-themed motifs for a unique greeting card.
Motif: Page 27.

A handkerchief personalized with an adorable doggy design makes a wonderful gift for fellow dog lovers.
Motif: Page 20.

Create an embroidered portrait of your own pup.
Motif: Page 23.

Tools & Materials

EMBROIDERY FLOSS

The designs in this book were created and stitched with DMC six strand embroidery floss 25 (Mouline Special 25). The six strands can be separated, which gives you the option to change the thickness of your stitches.

Embroidery floss packages are labeled with a color number. Metallic embroidery floss color numbers start with the letter E followed by a number.

These label numbers are coordinated with the stitch diagrams for each design in this book so it's easy figure out which colors you will need for each motif.

A few motifs in the book use DMC Size 12 floss which is heavier than regular embroidery floss and there are no threads to separate. It's good for covering larger areas.

NEEDLES

Embroidery needles have large eyes specifically designed to use with embroidery floss and their sharp tips travel through a variety of fabrics with ease. For the designs in this book, use needle sizes 3, 5, or 7. Use the chart below to choose proper size needle based on the number of threads you need to use for your motif.

The higher the needle size, the smaller the needle!

Needle Size	Number of Strands
No. 3	6
No. 5	3-4
No. 7	1-2

Size 7

Size 5

Size 3

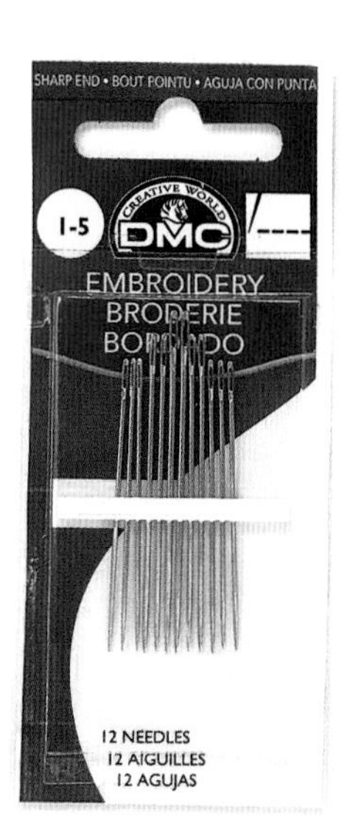

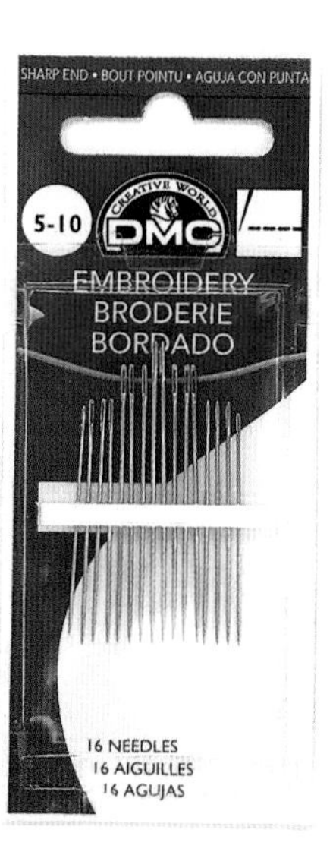

SCISSORS

Thread snips are used for cutting embroidery floss. Fabric shears are better for cutting embroidery fabric. Make sure your scissors are sharp.

FABRICS AND HOOPS

You can use pretty much any type of fabric for embroidery—cotton, linen, felt, or wool. Fabric made for embroidery will give you the best results because the weight and weave are designed specifically for that purpose.

An embroidery hoop holds the fabric taut while stitching and will help keep it from puckering. You can use a 4-6 inch (10-15 cm) hoop for most of the designs in this book.

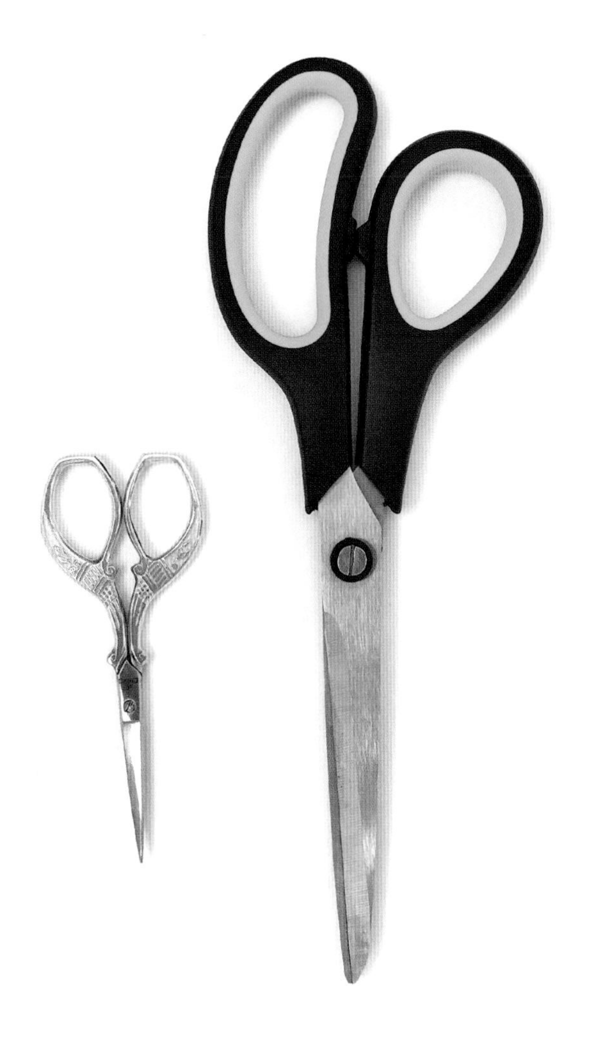

Left: Thread Snips
Right: Fabric Shears

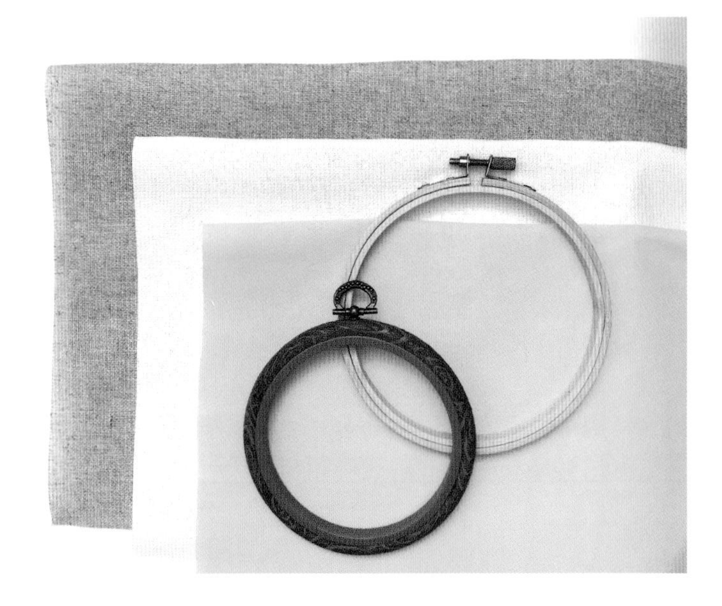

Basic Techniques

TRANSFERRING DESIGNS

1. Place a sheet of dressmaker's carbon paper in position over your fabric. Make sure the chalk side is down.
2. Use tracing paper to make a copy of the design you want to transfer. Place the tracing paper on top of the dressmaker's carbon paper.
3. Use a ballpoint pen or a stylus to trace over the motif.
4. When you press the pen or stylus, the chalk will transfer onto the fabric. If the transferred image isn't dark enough you can go over it with an aqua trick marker to darken the lines.

1

2

3

4

PREPARING EMBROIDERY FLOSS

1. Pull the loose end of the embroidery thread carefully from the package.
2. You can work with the skein or instead wrap the threads onto a cardboard bobbin, which helps avoid tangles.
3. Cut a length about 16-20 inches (40-50 cm) long.
4. Divide the thread into individual strands.
5. Align the number of threads you need together. Even if you are using 6 threads, you should divide all the threads first and then recombine them together. There is less chance the threads will knot.

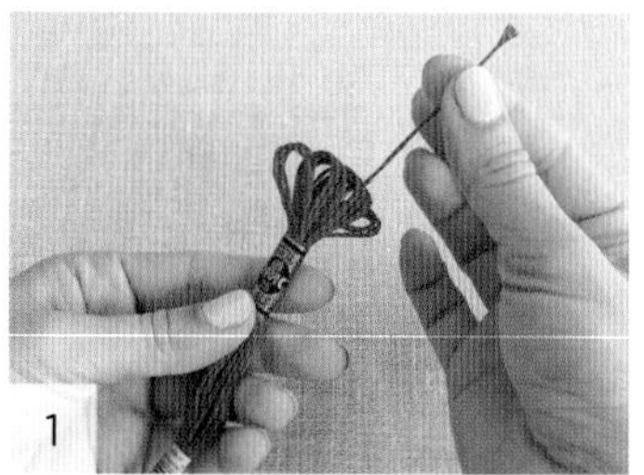
1

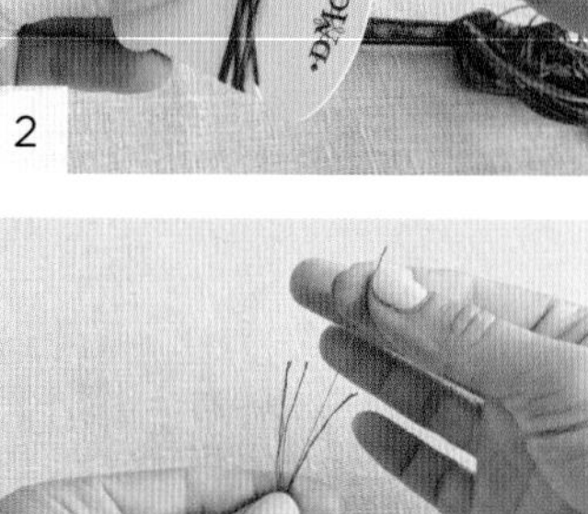
2

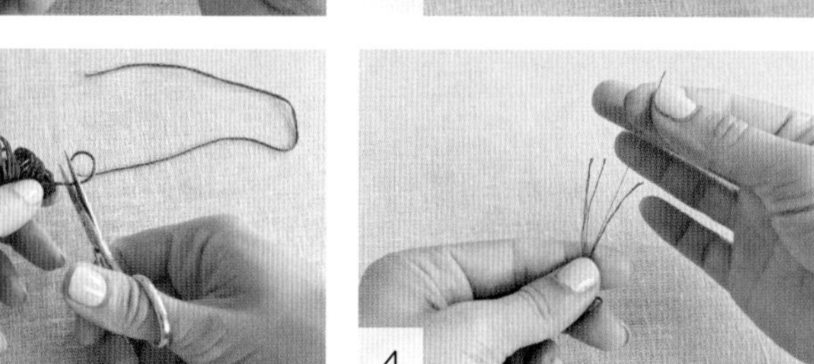
3

4

5

THREADING THE NEEDLE

1. Bend the thread into a fold that's about 1 inch (2.5 cm) long. Use the needle to hold the thread taut which will help create a crease.
2. Push the fold through the eye of the needle.
3. Pull the folded part the rest of the way through the eye of the needle.
4. Leave about a 4 inch (10 cm) tail from the needle.

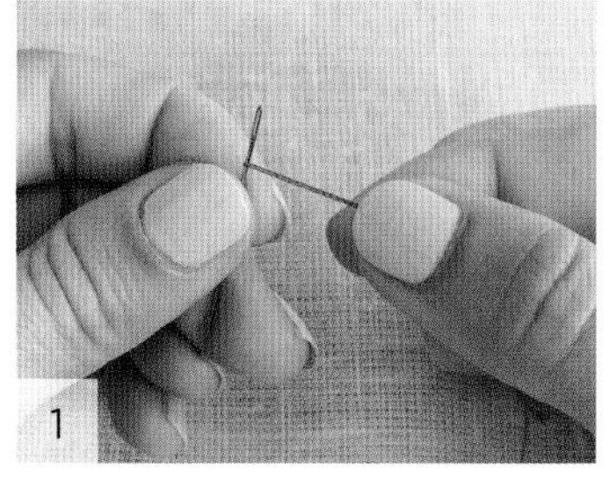

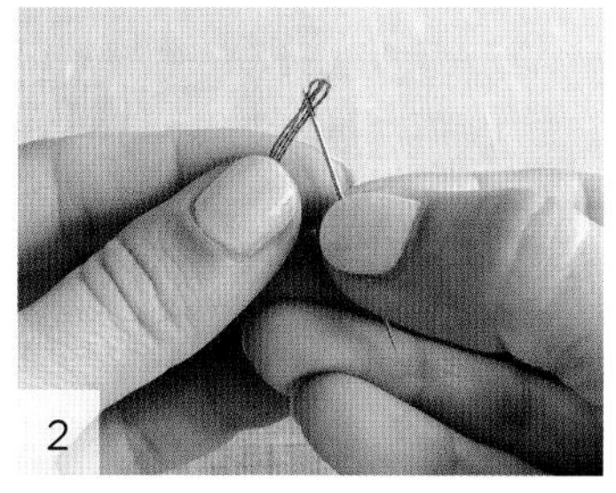

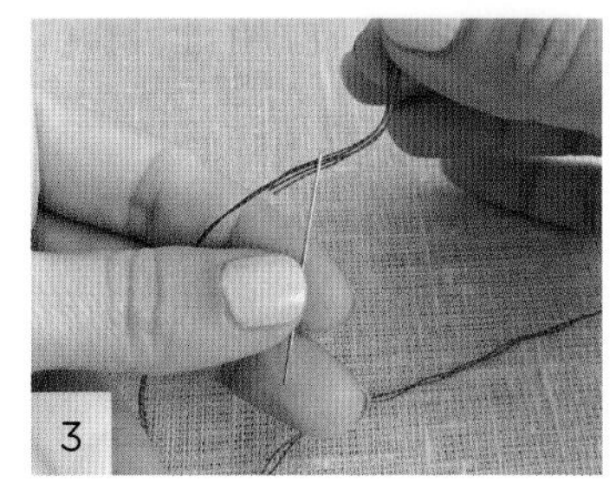

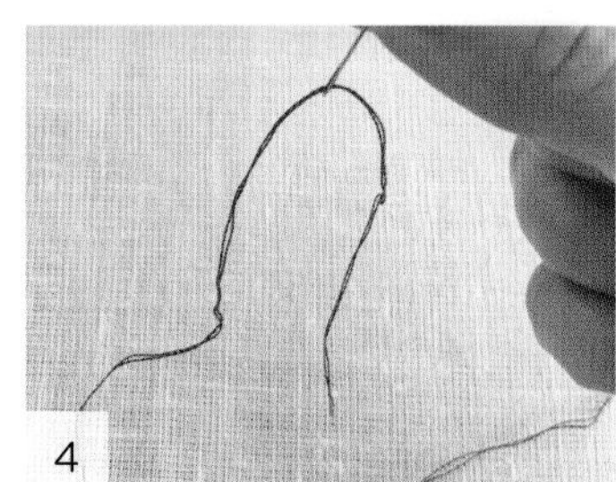

MAKING KNOTS

1. Place the needle at the end of the length of floss.
2. Wrap the floss around the needle two times.
3. With the fingers of one hand, hold onto the wrapped threads. With your other hand, pull the needle out, while holding onto the wrapped threads. Pull the wrapped threads toward the end of your length of floss to create a knot.
4. Your finished knot should look like this.

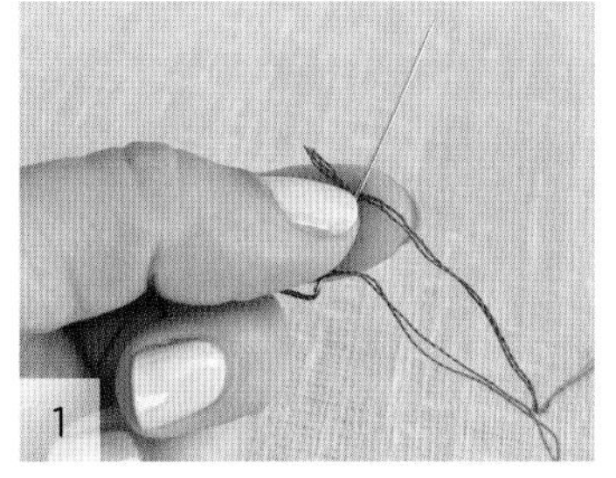

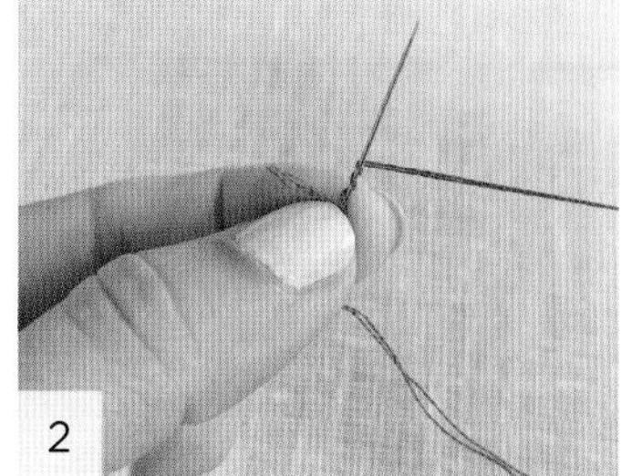

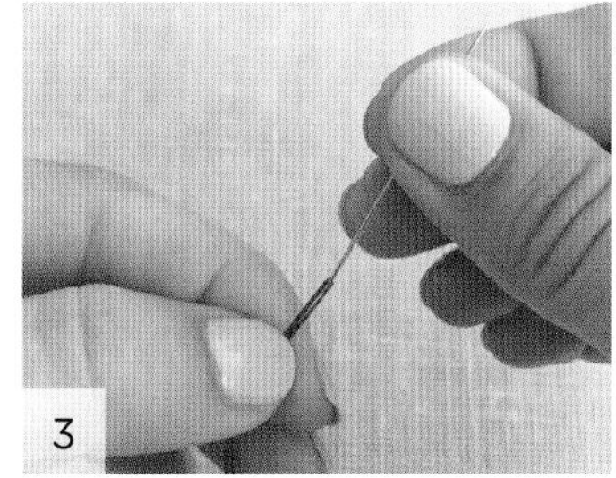

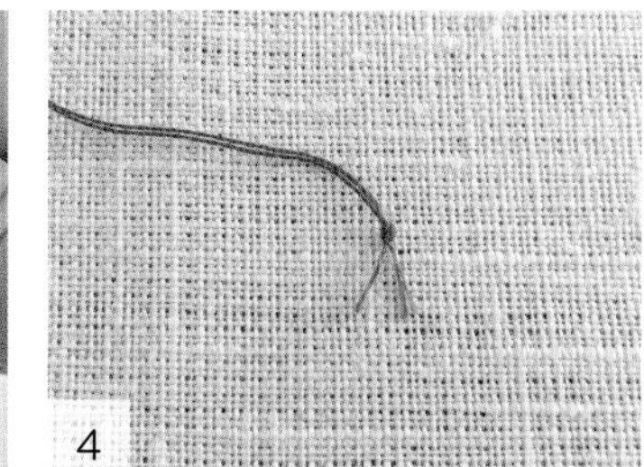

FINISHING

1. Place your needle as shown over the top of the stitches on the wrong side of the fabric.
2. Wrap the embroidery floss around the needle two times.
3. Hold the wrapped thread against the fabric with a finger. With your other hand, pull the needle out of the fabric.
4. Your finished knot should look like this.

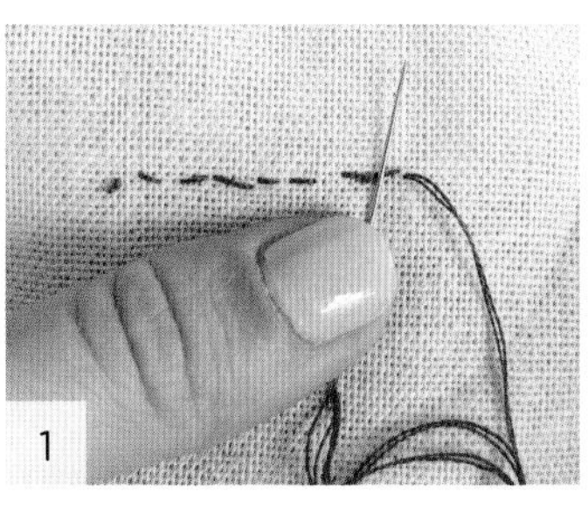

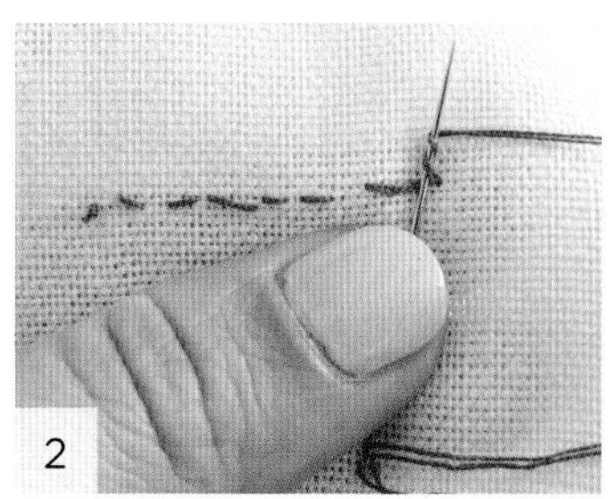

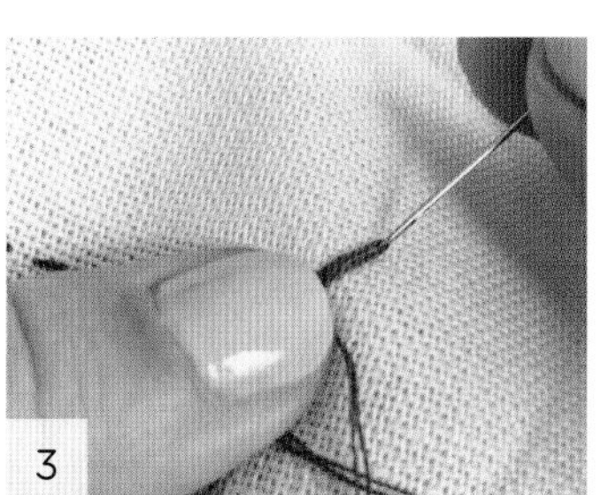

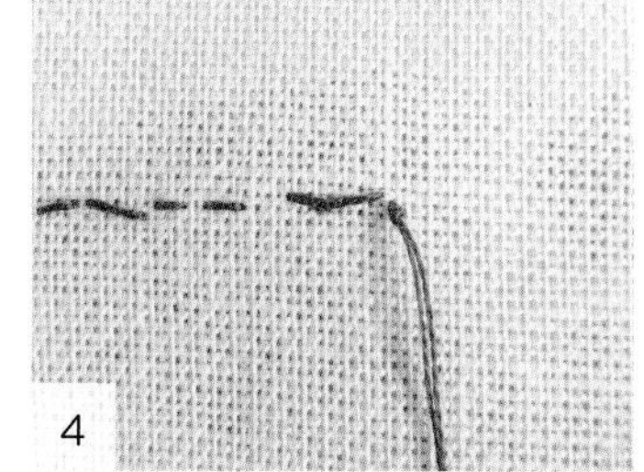

Right Side / Wrong Side

The look of the wrong side of your embroidery piece can affect the look of the right side so keep these tips in mind:

- Begin and finish your stitches as instructed on page 45 to avoid any bumps or long threads disturbing the look of your finished piece.
- If you need to move to a new area to stitch, start a new thread or run the needle behind other threads, or the thread might show on the right side, particularly if you are working with dark thread on a light fabric.

The following photos show the right and wrong sides of finished motifs.

RIGHT SIDE | WRONG SIDE

Design & Stitching: MakikoArt (Oksana Kokovkina)

Using Embroidery Floss

The embroidery floss used in this book has six strands. When you separate and combine them in different numbers, your stitches and final motifs will have a variety of thicknesses. Each design in the book indicates how many strands you should use for each stitch. The images here show how different your stitches could look depending on the number of strands you stitch with.

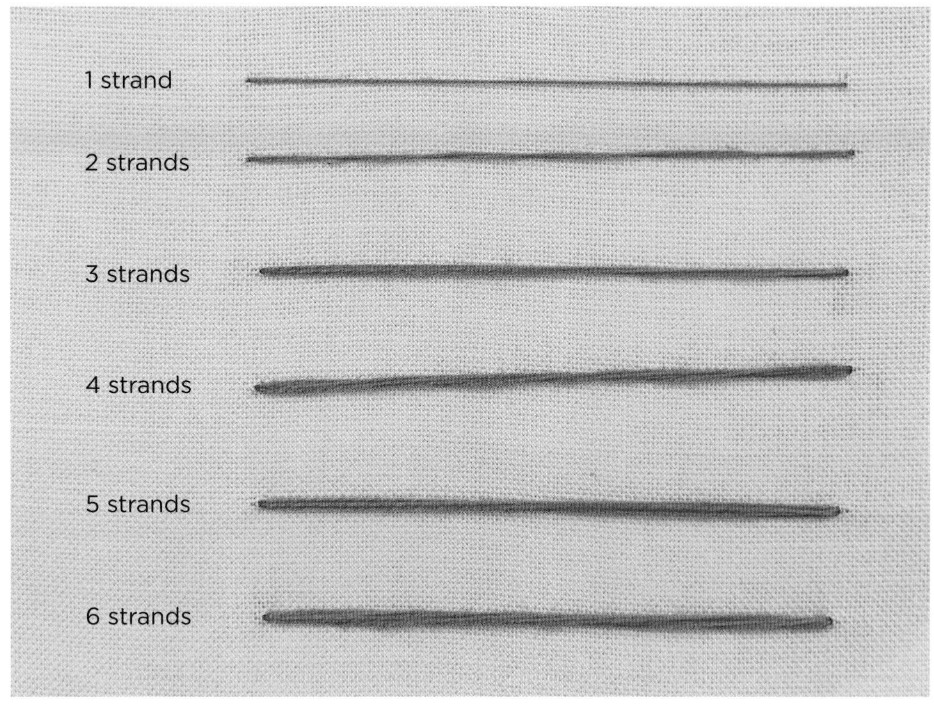

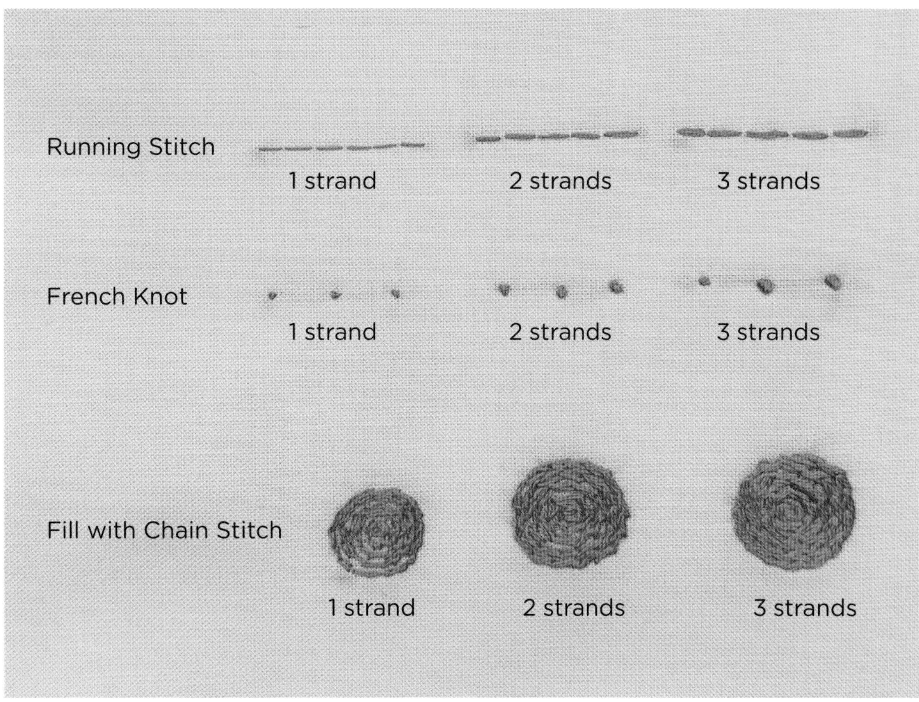

Basic Stitch Guide

BACKSTITCH (BS)

Pull the needle out at 1 and push it in through 2. This makes one stitch. Pull the needle back up at 3 and push it in through 1. We are creating a stitch by taking the thread backward. Pull the needle out at 4 and push it in through 3. Continue this pattern to finish your design. For curved lines and shapes you can make the stitches shorter.

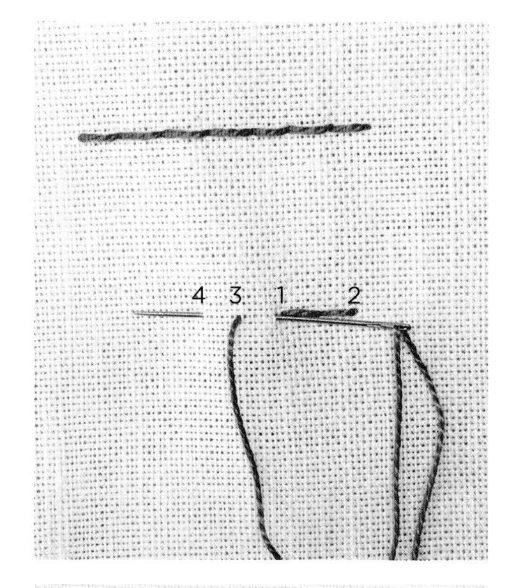

BLANKET STITCH (BL)

A. Pull the needle out at 1. Pull the thread so it extends horizontally to the right. Push in the needle at 2 and pull it out at 3, which is parallel to 1. Be sure to keep the thread under the needle.

B. Make the next stitch by pulling the thread to the right and insert the needle at 4, which is parallel to 2. Pull the needle out at 5, which is parallel to 1 and 3. Be sure to keep the floss under the needle.

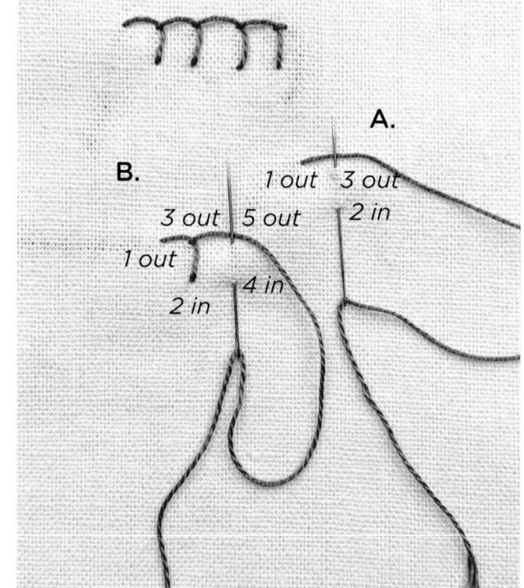

BULLION KNOT (BK)

A. Pull the needle out at 1 which will become the top of the knot. Push the needle in at 2 and pull the needle out at 3 (the same hole as 1).

B. Wrap the thread around the needle as many times as your motif requires. Use your fingers to secure the wraps against the fabric and pull the needle out.

C. Push the needle back in through 2 and tighten the knot against the fabric.

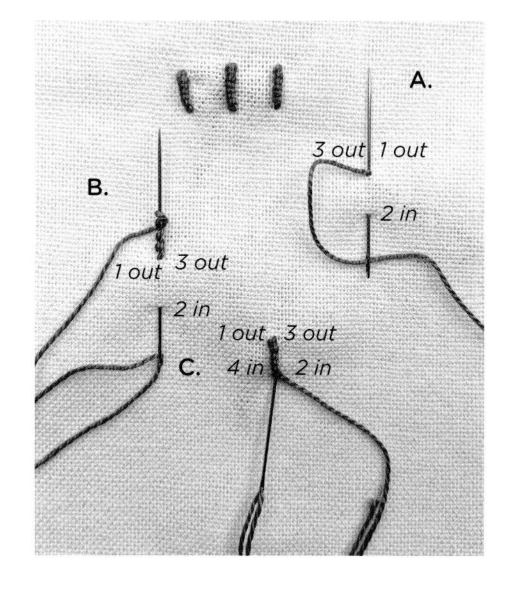

CHAIN STITCH (CH)

A. Pull the needle out at 1. Wrap the thread around the tip of the needle as shown. Push in the needle at 1 and immediately pull the needle out again at 2.

B. Pull the needle and thread until a small loop remains. This is a finished chain. Push the needle back through the same hole at 2. Use the same technique to pull the needle and thread out at 3 to complete the next chain.

C. To finish a row, push the needle back through the fabric and make a very small straight stitch which will secure the last chain, as shown by 4.

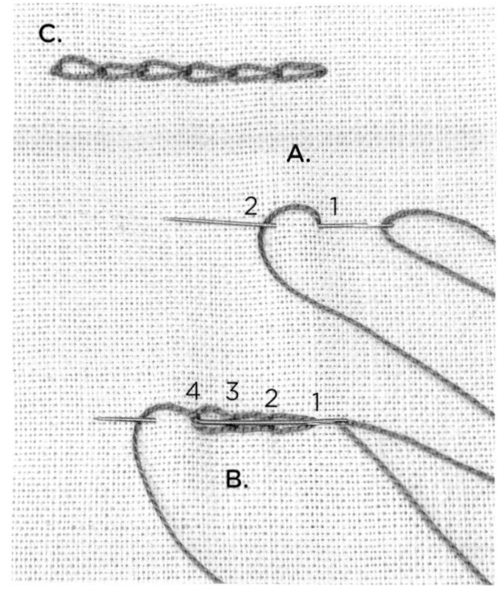

COUCHING STITCH (CS)

We've used two different colors of thread to illustrate how to work the couching stitch. Individual instructions for colors will vary.

A. Pull the main floss color out at X, then rest it along the motif line. Pull the second thread color out at 1. Push in at 2, right below 1, and make a very small straight stitch to secure the main thread in place. Pull the needle out at 3.

B. Keep making very small, evenly spaced straight stitches to hold the main thread in place along the motif line. To finish, insert the main thread color back through the fabric at Y.

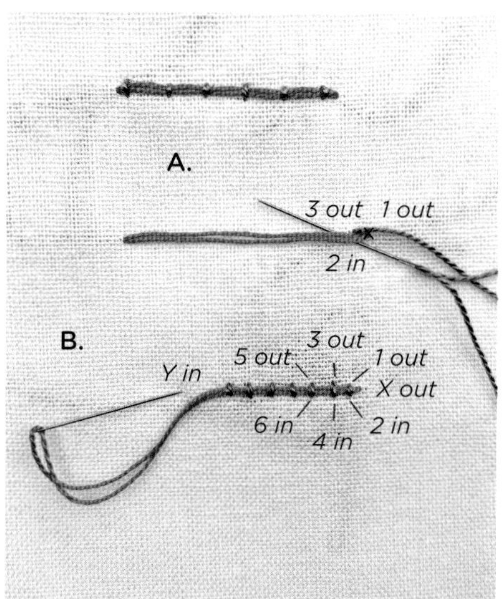

CROSS STITCH (CR)

Cross stitches can be made from bottom to top, or top to bottom.

A. Pull the needle out at 1. Push the needle at 2, making a diagonal stitch. Pull the needle out at 3, parallel to 2.

B. Push the needle in at 4, which will complete the cross.

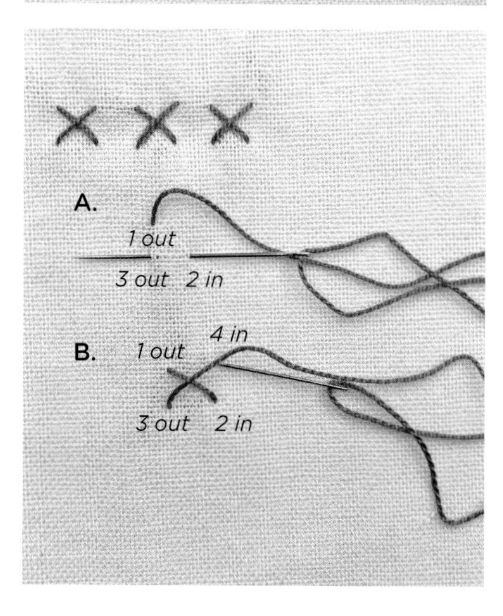

FISHBONE STITCH (FI)

A. Pull the needle out at 1, which is at the point of the design. Push the needle in at 2 the center spine of the design. Draw the needle out at 3 along the left edge of the design.

B. Push the needle in at 4, which is next to 2. Pull the needle out at 5 along the right outline of the design.

C. Push the needle in at 6, just beneath 4 and 5. Pull the needle out at 7. Continue to work diagonal stitches from the spine of the design.

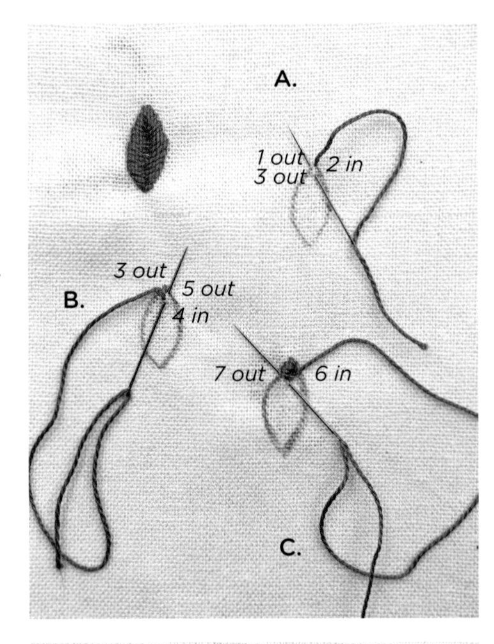

FLY STITCH (FS)

A. Pull the needle out at 1. Pull the thread down at an angle and insert the needle at 2, as shown. Pull the needle out at 3.

B. Pull the thread through the fabric to form a V-shaped stitch. Make a very small straight stitch to secure the V by pushing in the needle at 4, right underneath 3.

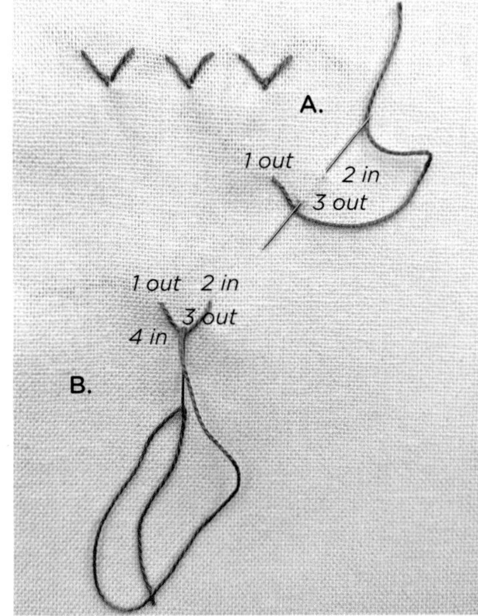

FRENCH KNOT (FK)

Pull the needle out through 1. Place the needle close to the fabric. Wrap the thread around it twice, as shown. Hold the longer end of the thread taut with your fingers while pushing the needle back in at a point close to 1 or even into 1. Push the needle down through the fabric and pull tight.

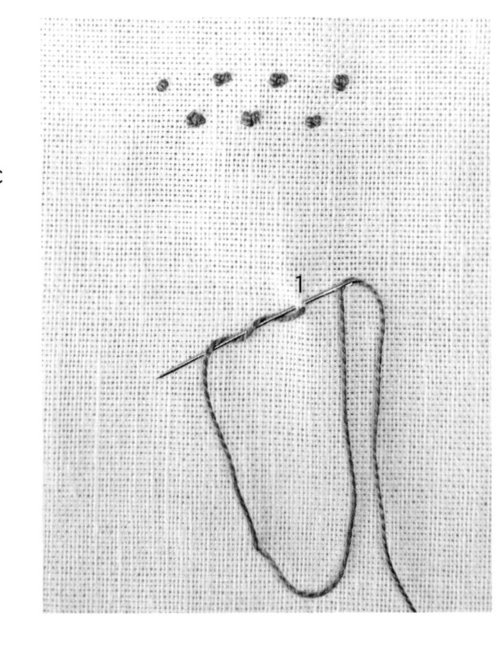

LAZY DAISY STITCH (LD)

A. Pull the needle out at 1. Wrap the floss around the needle tip as shown. Push the needle in at 2 (this is actually the same hole as 1), then pull the needle out at 3.

B. Pull the needle and floss through the fabric until a small loop remains. Insert the needle at 4, making a tiny straight stitch to secure the loop.

C. This is the same technique used to make a chain stitch but each stitch is finished with a straight stitch.

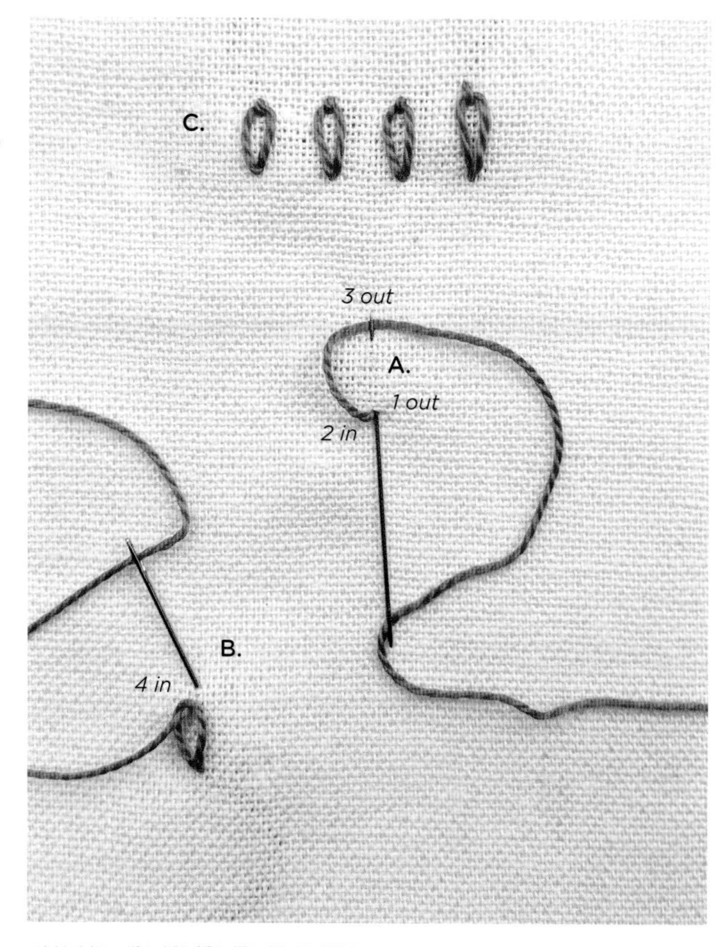

LONG AND SHORT STITCHES (LS)

A. Pull the needle out at 1. Push the needle in at 2 and pull the needle out at 3.

B. The distance from 2 to 3 should be shorter than the distance from 1 to 2. This will give you the long and short stitches you are looking for.

C. Continue altering long and short stitches.

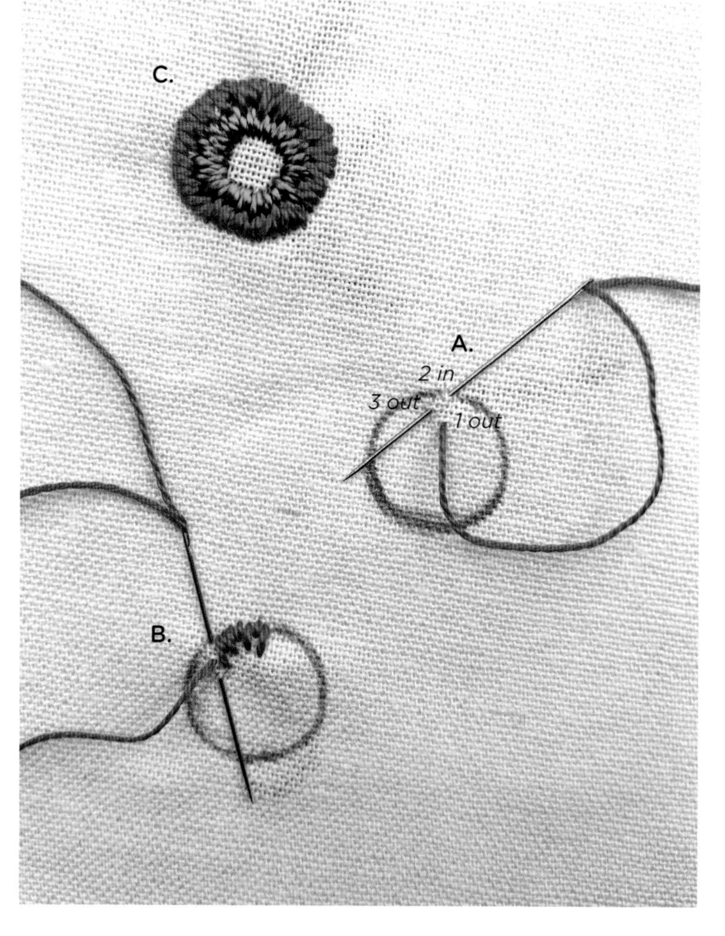

OUTLINE STITCH (OU)

Work this stitch from left to right.

A. Pull the needle out at 1. Insert the needle at 2 and pull the needle out again at 3, which should be halfway between 1 and 2.

B. Continue stitching by inserting the needle at 4. Pull the needle out at 5, which should be halfway between 3 and 4. This is a very handy stitch for straight and curved outlines.

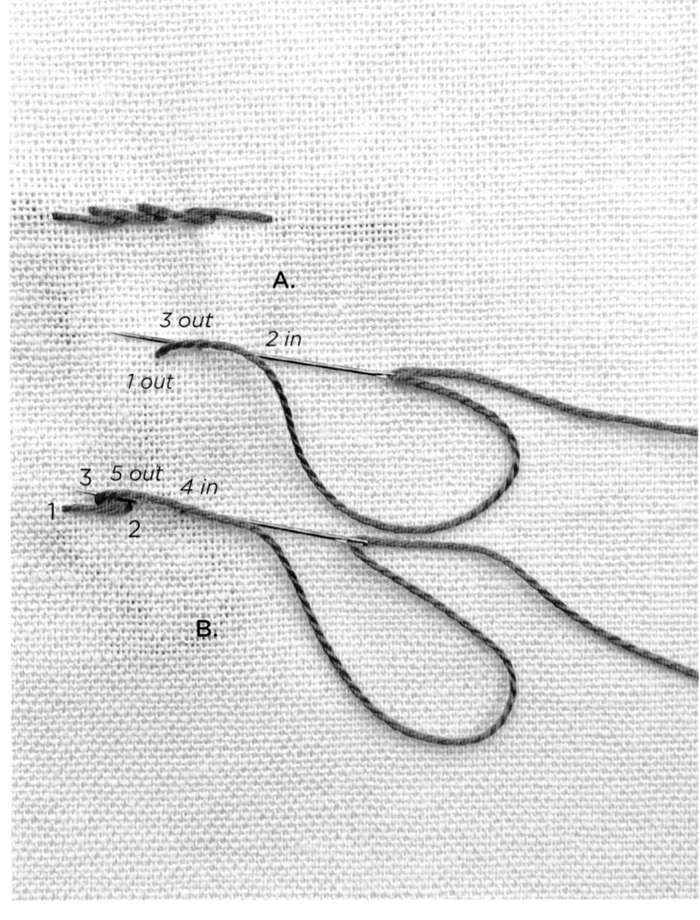

RUNNING STITCH (RU)

Pull the needle through from the back to the front of the fabric at point 1 and push the needle from the front to the back at 2 to finish the stitch. Pull the needle up again at 3 and push down at 4.

Create different looks by altering the length of the spaces between the stitches. This stitch can be worked in straight or curved lines.

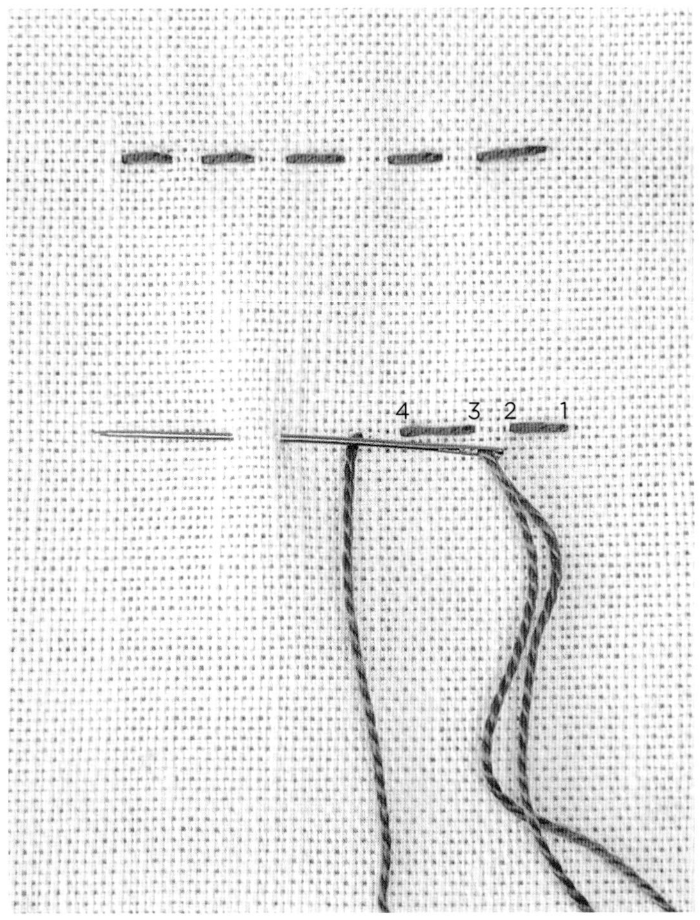

SATIN STITCH (SA)

Pull the needle out through 1 and push it in through 2. Pull the needle up through 3, right next to point 1. Continue this technique over the two stitch lines. The finished stitch will fill in the area as shown.

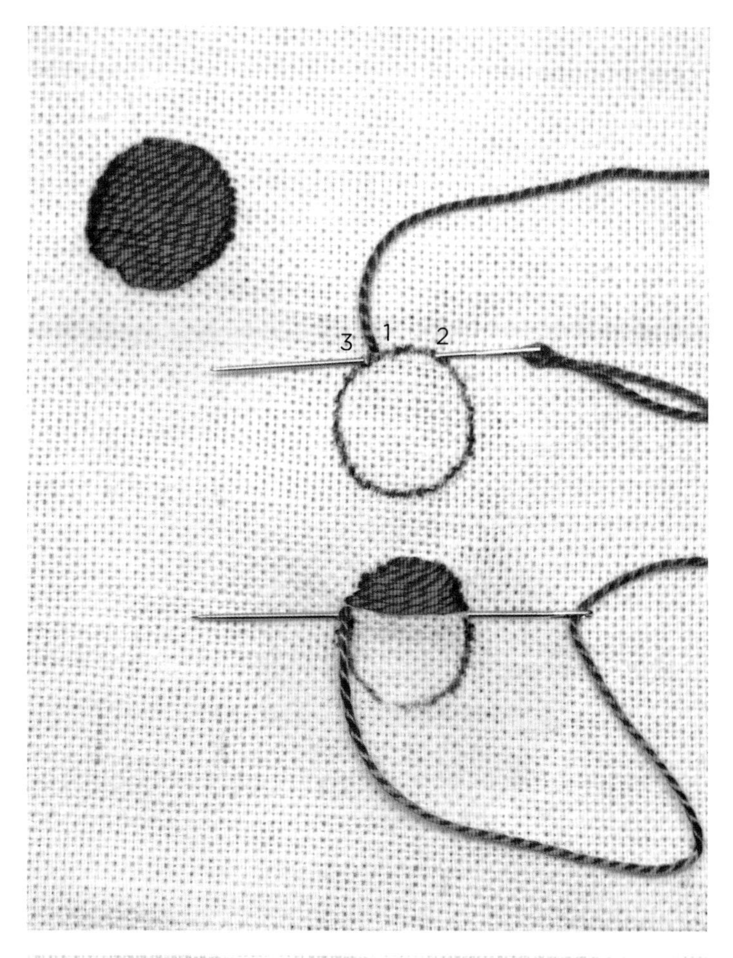

STRAIGHT STITCH (ST)

A. Pull the needle out at 1 and immediately insert at 2. That makes one straight stitch.

B. Continue making stitches by pulling the needle out at 3 and then inserting at 4. Continue by following the technique.

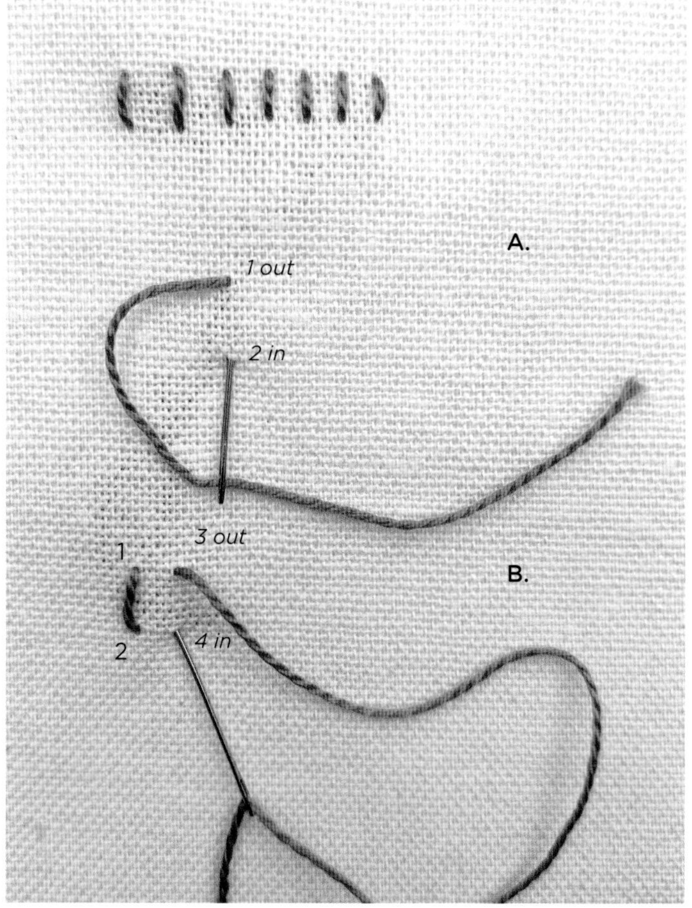

Using This Book

The motifs in this book each have a stitch guide that includes everything you'll need to complete the design plus a full-size template to use for tracing the motif and transferring it to your fabric. At the top of each page, there is also information that gives specific details about the motifs on that page. Read these tips to understand the embroidery diagrams.

A. **Motif Number:** Use this number to find the design in the book. The number is cross referenced on the photos of the stitched motifs at the beginning of the book.

B. **Stitch Name:** These indicate which stitch you should use for each element of the design. Refer to the Basic Stitch Guide on pages 48–53 to learn how to make each of the 15 basic stitches used in the book.

C. **Number of Strands:** Numbers within circles (#) indicate how many strands of embroidery thread to use for a particular stitch.

D. **Color Number:** The color of the embroidery thread is indicated with a 3 or 4 digit number. DMC brand was used to stitch all the designs in this book.

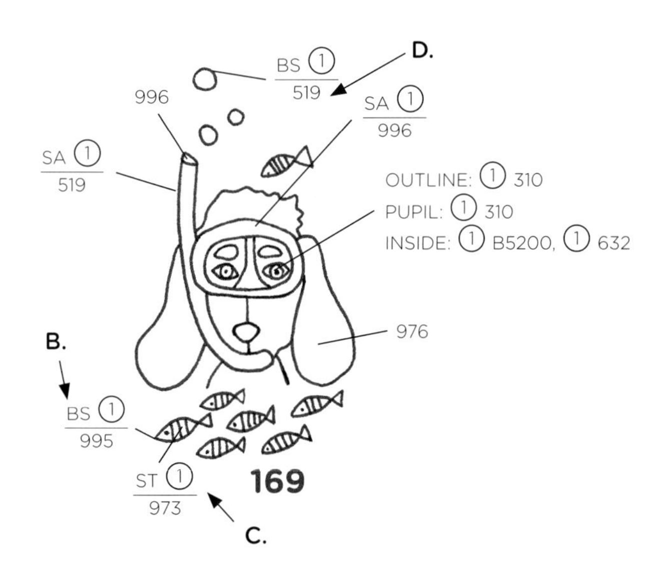

Customizing Motifs

The motifs in the book have stitch guides so you can reproduce the motif in the exact colors, but that's really just a jumping-off point. Feel free to change a few colors and create a motif of your own dog!

Creating a stitched motif of your own dog is simple. Choose a motif from the book that most closely looks like your dog and then choose thread colors to match your pup. In this example, you can see that by changing the color of the thread and using short and long stitches instead of satin stitches, a small cocoa brown dog turns into a fluffy white pup.

All-Time Favorites

Motifs: Page 6
Design & Stitching: Insanitynice (Valentina Castillo Mora)

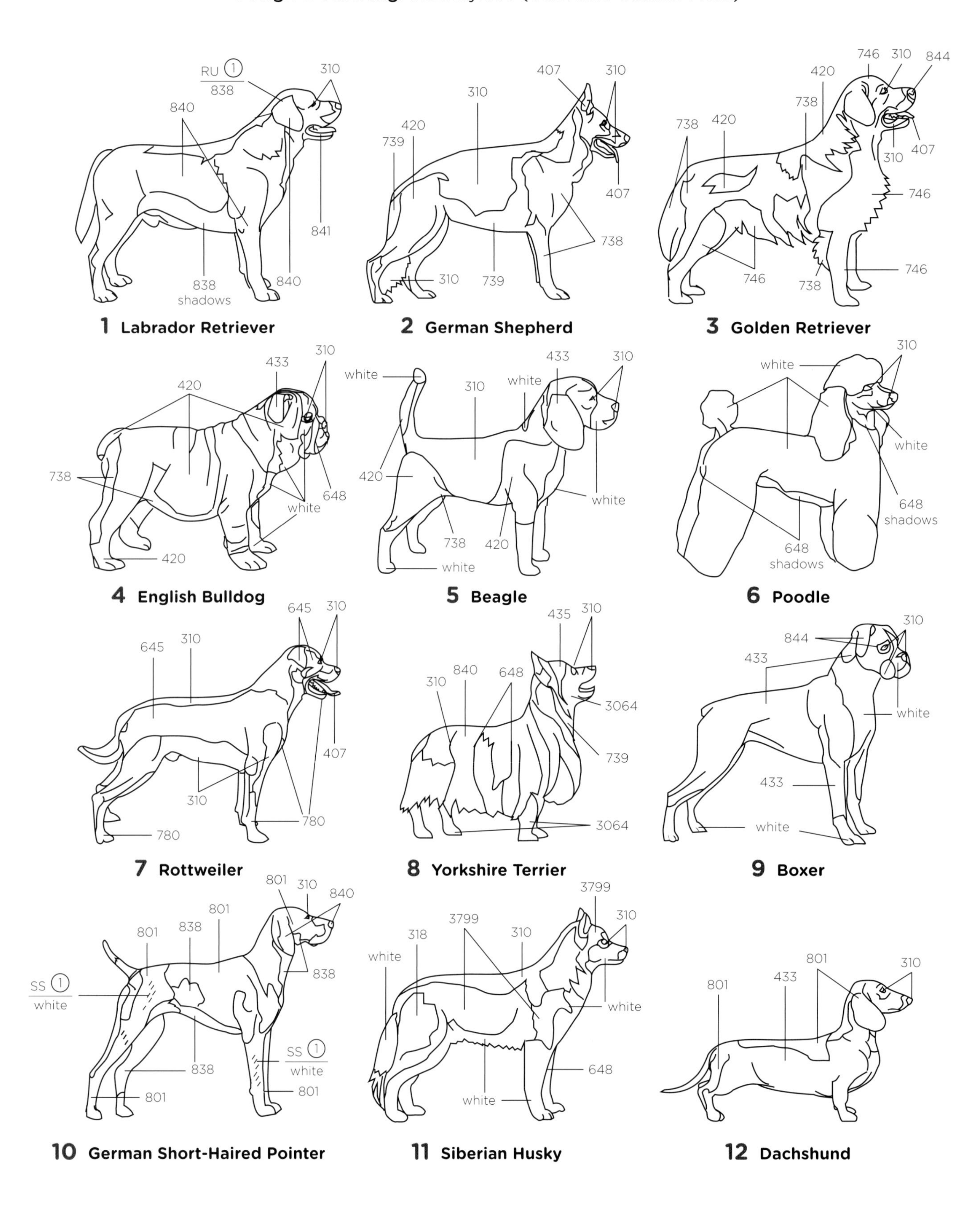

1 Labrador Retriever
2 German Shepherd
3 Golden Retriever
4 English Bulldog
5 Beagle
6 Poodle
7 Rottweiler
8 Yorkshire Terrier
9 Boxer
10 German Short-Haired Pointer
11 Siberian Husky
12 Dachshund

- Use 1 strand unless indicated with (#)
- # indicates color number
- Use Long and Short stitches unless otherwise indicated

All-Time Favorites

Motifs: Page 7
Design & Stitching: Insanitynice (Valentina Castillo Mora)

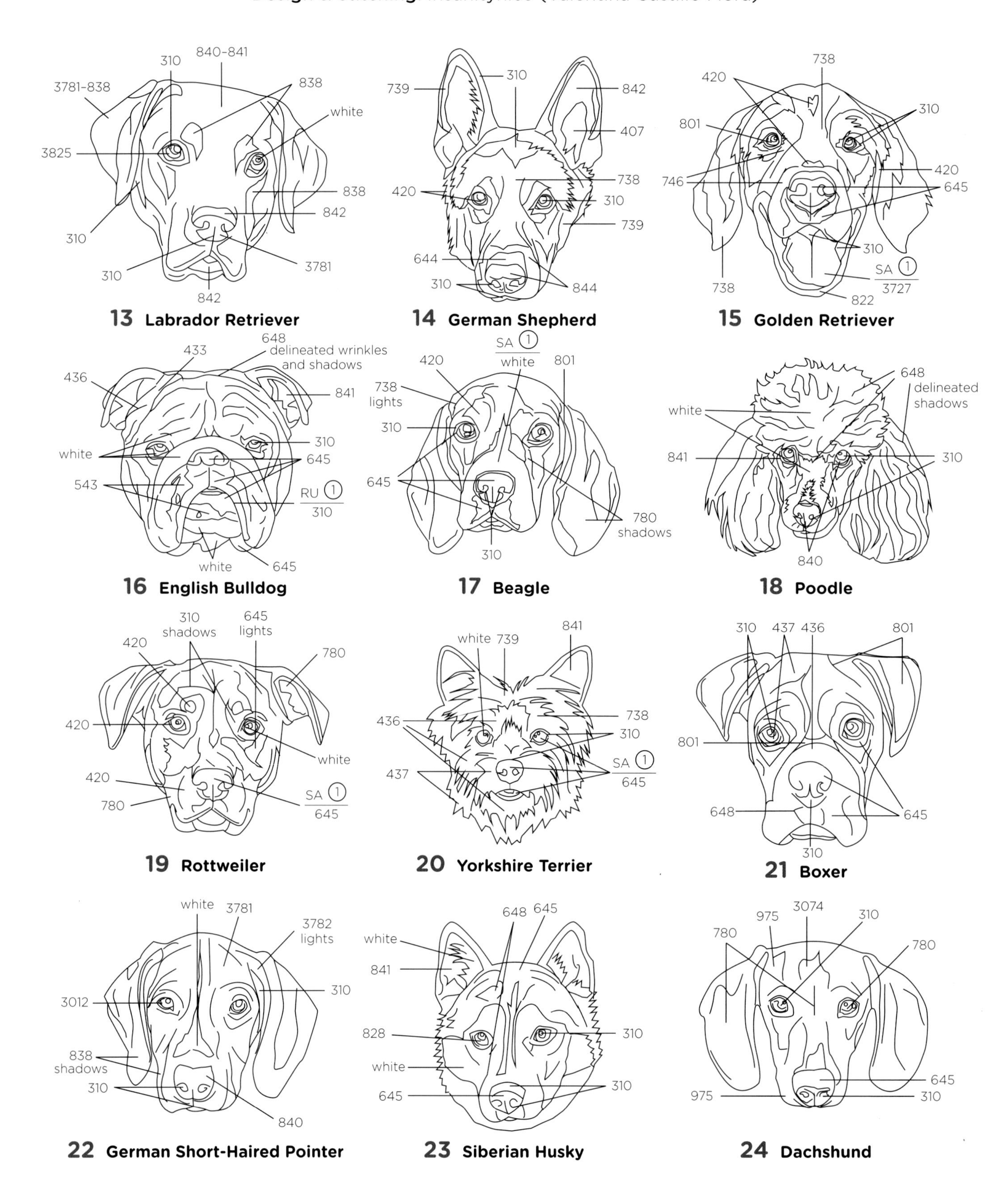

13 Labrador Retriever

14 German Shepherd

15 Golden Retriever

16 English Bulldog

17 Beagle

18 Poodle

19 Rottweiler

20 Yorkshire Terrier

21 Boxer

22 German Short-Haired Pointer

23 Siberian Husky

24 Dachshund

- Use 1 strand unless indicated with (#) ▪ # indicates color number
- Use Long and Short stitches unless otherwise indicated

Little Friends

Motifs: Page 8

Design & Stitching: Insanitynice (Valentina Castillo Mora)

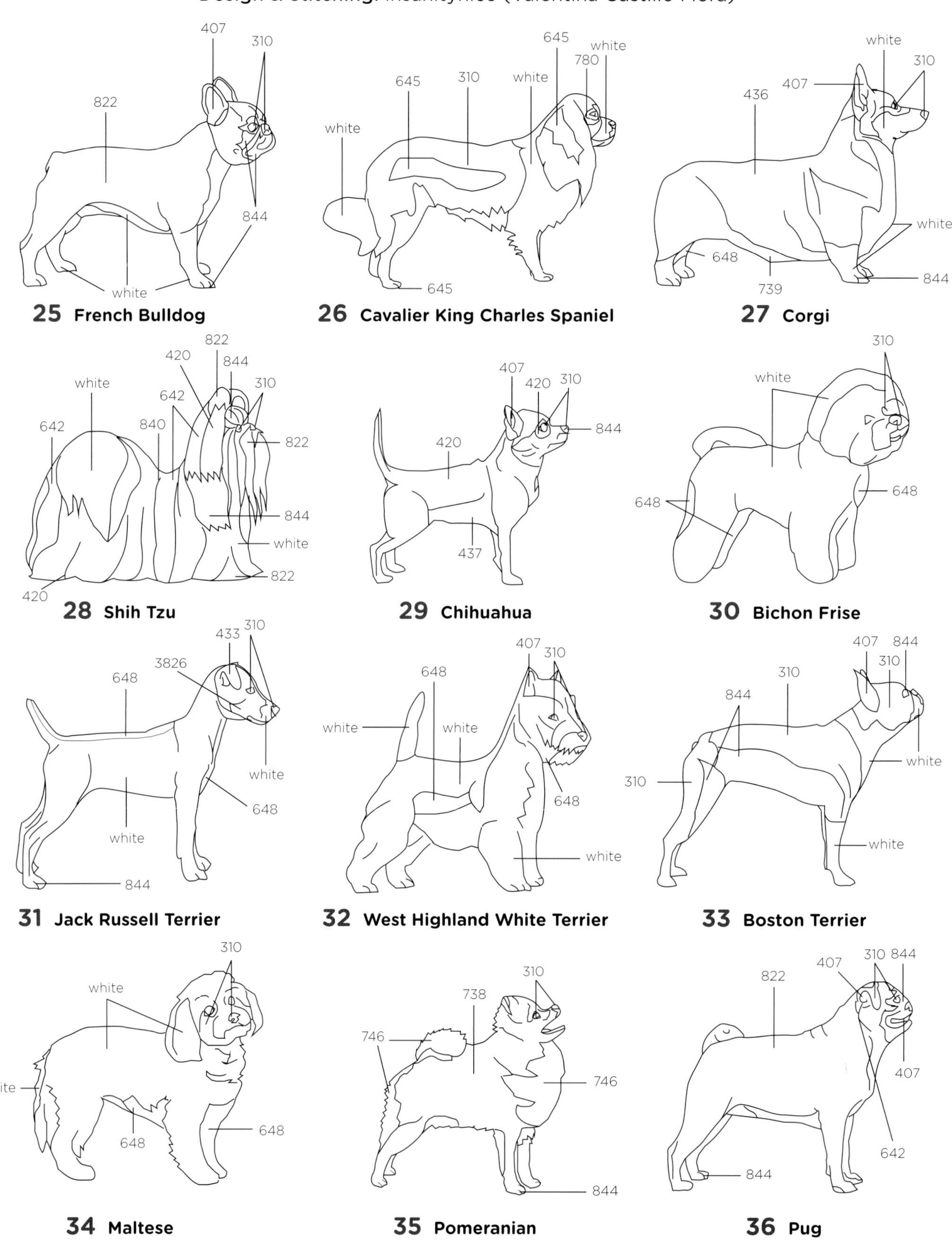

25 French Bulldog

26 Cavalier King Charles Spaniel

27 Corgi

28 Shih Tzu

29 Chihuahua

30 Bichon Frise

31 Jack Russell Terrier

32 West Highland White Terrier

33 Boston Terrier

34 Maltese

35 Pomeranian

36 Pug

- Use 1 strand unless indicated with (#)
- # indicates color number
- Fill areas with Long and Short stitches unless otherwise indicated

Little Friends

Motifs: Page 9
Design & Stitching: Insanitynice (Valentina Castillo Mora)

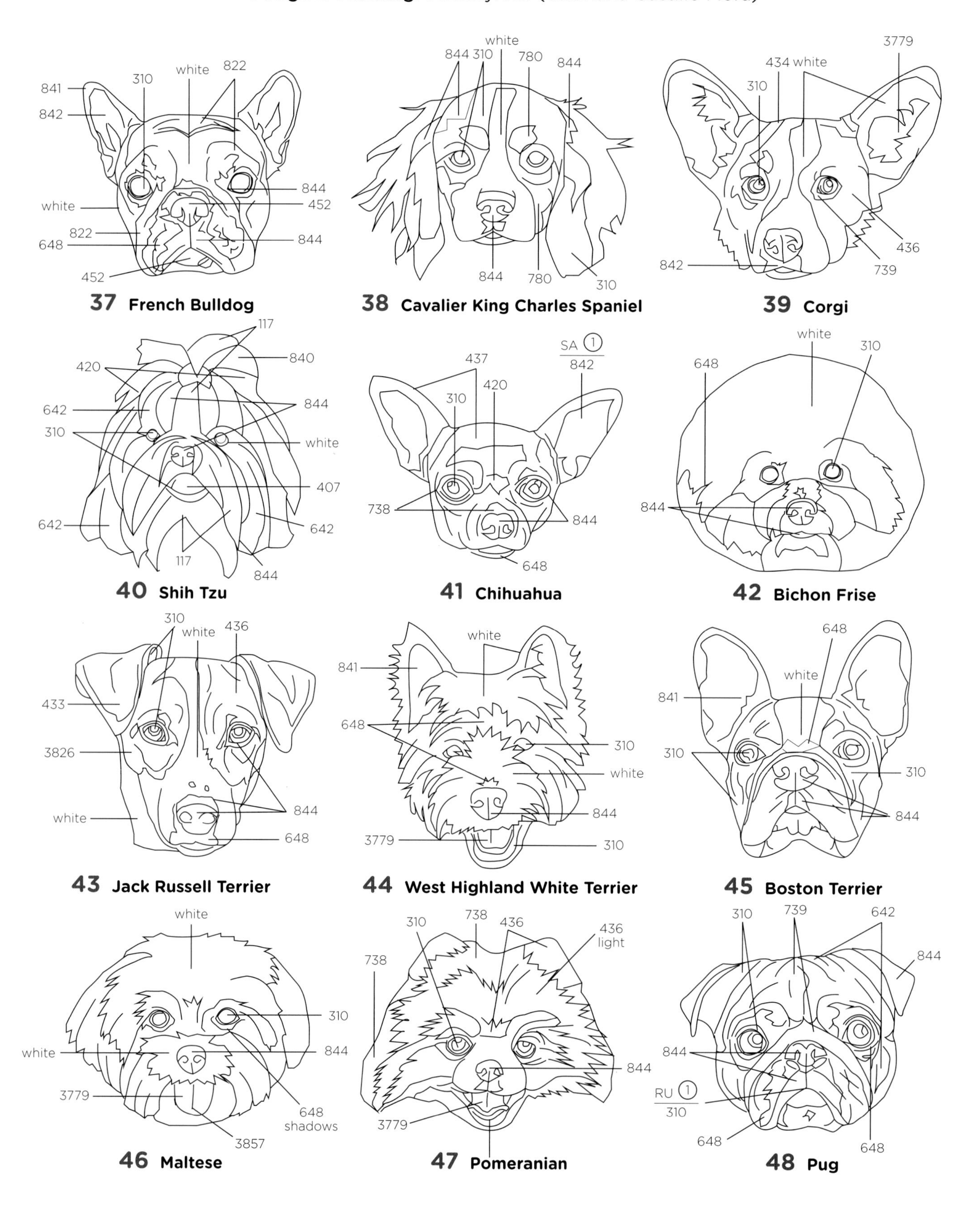

- Use 1 strand unless indicated with (#)
- # indicates color number
- Fill areas with Long and Short stitches unless otherwise indicated

37 French Bulldog

38 Cavalier King Charles Spaniel

39 Corgi

40 Shih Tzu

41 Chihuahua

42 Bichon Frise

43 Jack Russell Terrier

44 West Highland White Terrier

45 Boston Terrier

46 Maltese

47 Pomeranian

48 Pug

Big Friends

Motifs: Page 10
Design & Stitching: Insanitynice (Valentina Castillo Mora)

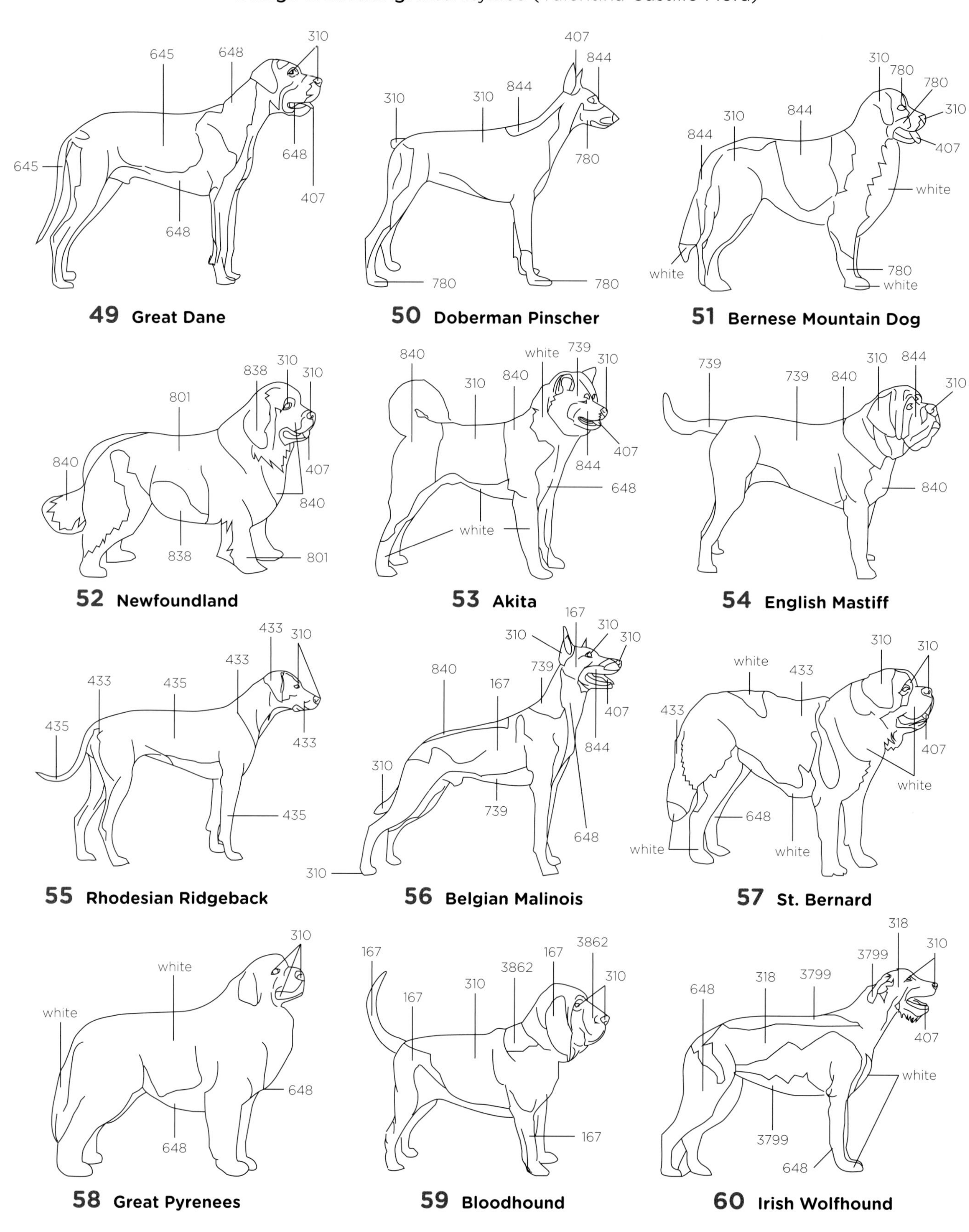

49 **Great Dane**
50 **Doberman Pinscher**
51 **Bernese Mountain Dog**
52 **Newfoundland**
53 **Akita**
54 **English Mastiff**
55 **Rhodesian Ridgeback**
56 **Belgian Malinois**
57 **St. Bernard**
58 **Great Pyrenees**
59 **Bloodhound**
60 **Irish Wolfhound**

- Use 1 strand unless indicated with (#)
- # indicates color number
- Fill areas with Long and Short stitches unless otherwise indicated

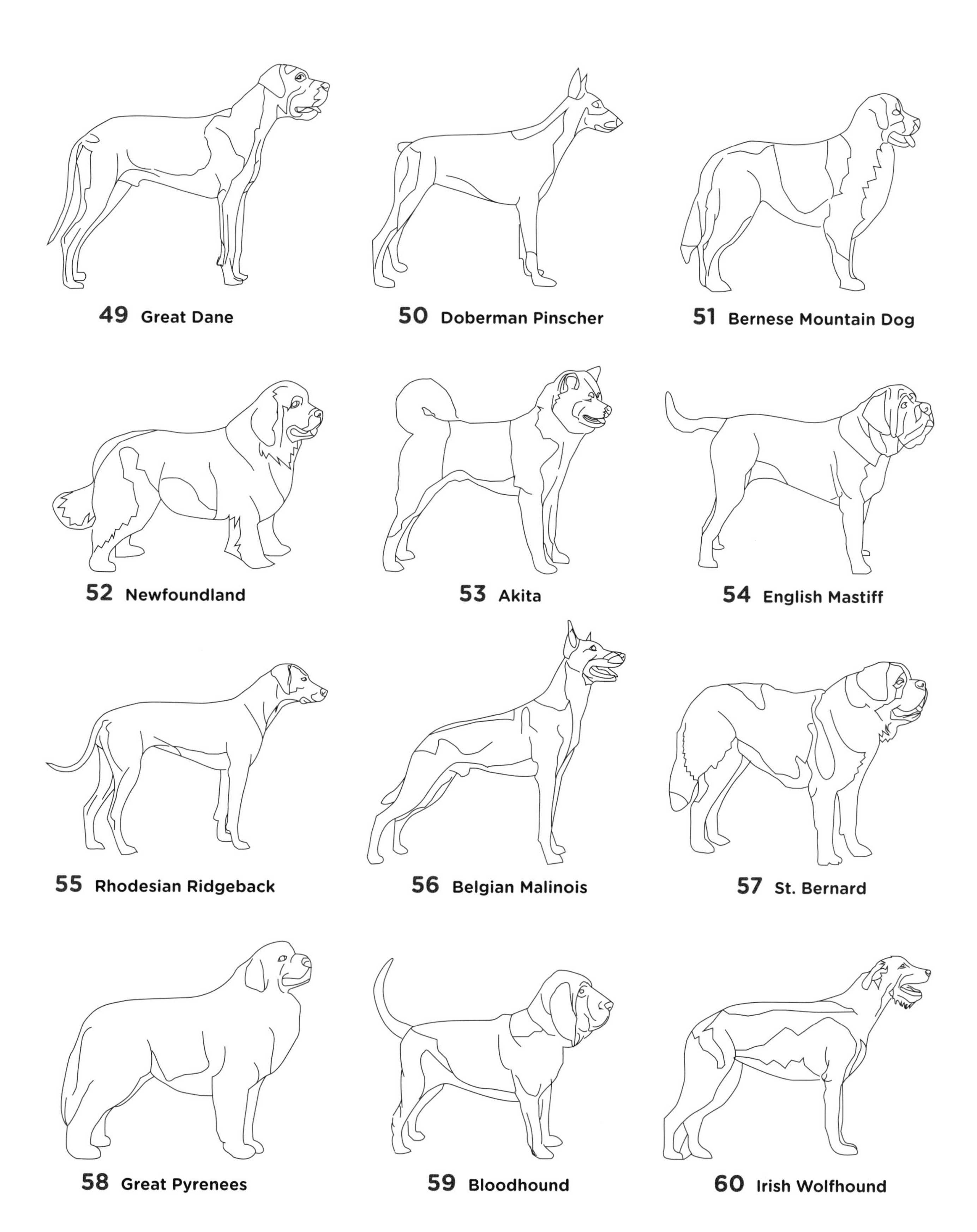

Big Friends

Motifs: Page 11
Design & Stitching: Insanitynice (Valentina Castillo Mora)

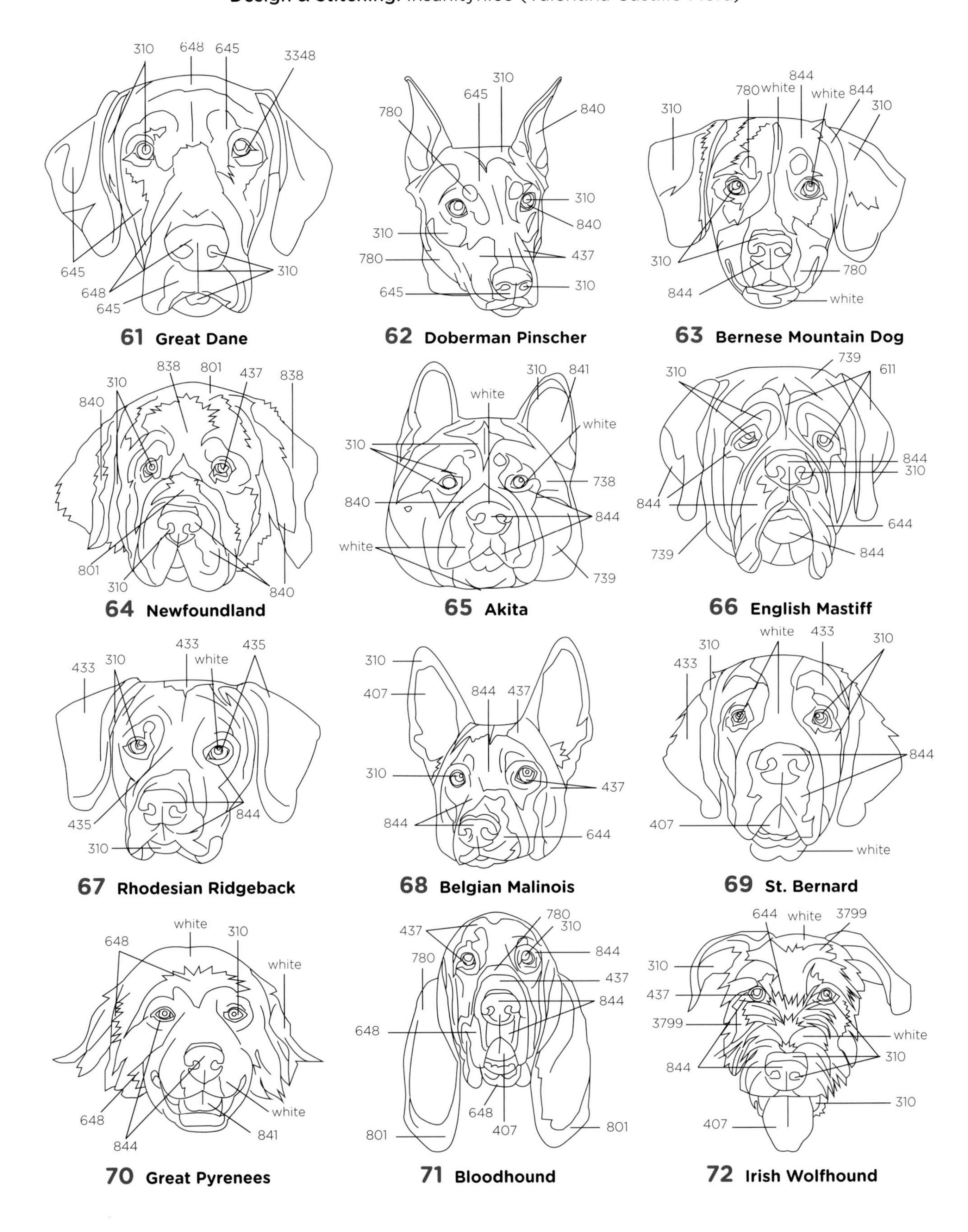

- Use 1 strand unless indicated with (#) ▪ # indicates color number
- Fill areas with Long and Short stitches unless otherwise indicated

61 Great Dane
62 Doberman Pinscher
63 Bernese Mountain Dog
64 Newfoundland
65 Akita
66 English Mastiff
67 Rhodesian Ridgeback
68 Belgian Malinois
69 St. Bernard
70 Great Pyrenees
71 Bloodhound
72 Irish Wolfhound

More to Love

Motifs: Page 12
Design & Stitching: Insanitynice (Valentina Castillo Mora)

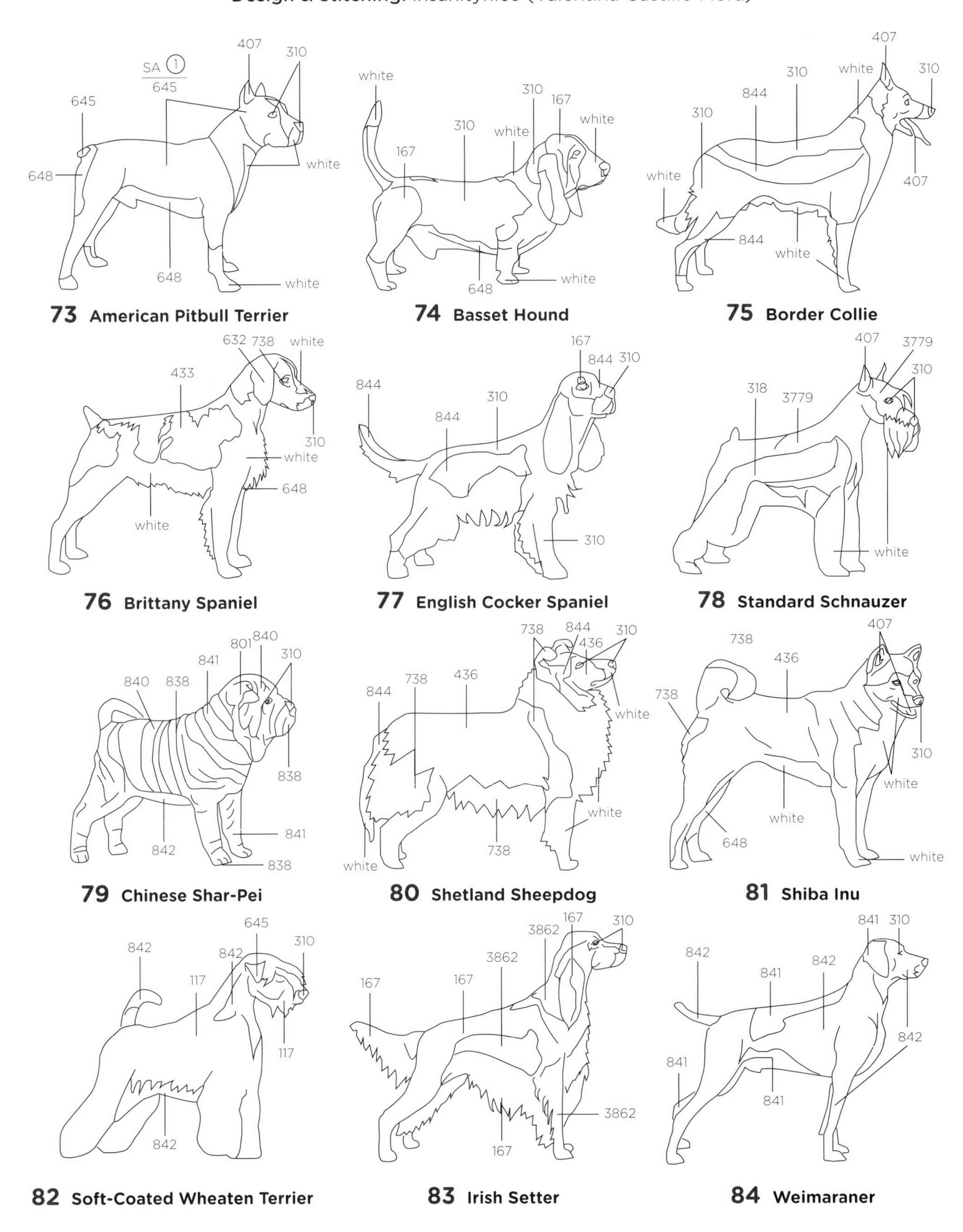

- Use 1 strand unless indicated with (#)
- # indicates color number
- Fill areas with Long and Short stitches unless otherwise indicated

More to Love

Motifs: Page 13
Design & Stitching: Insanitynice (Valentina Castillo Mora)

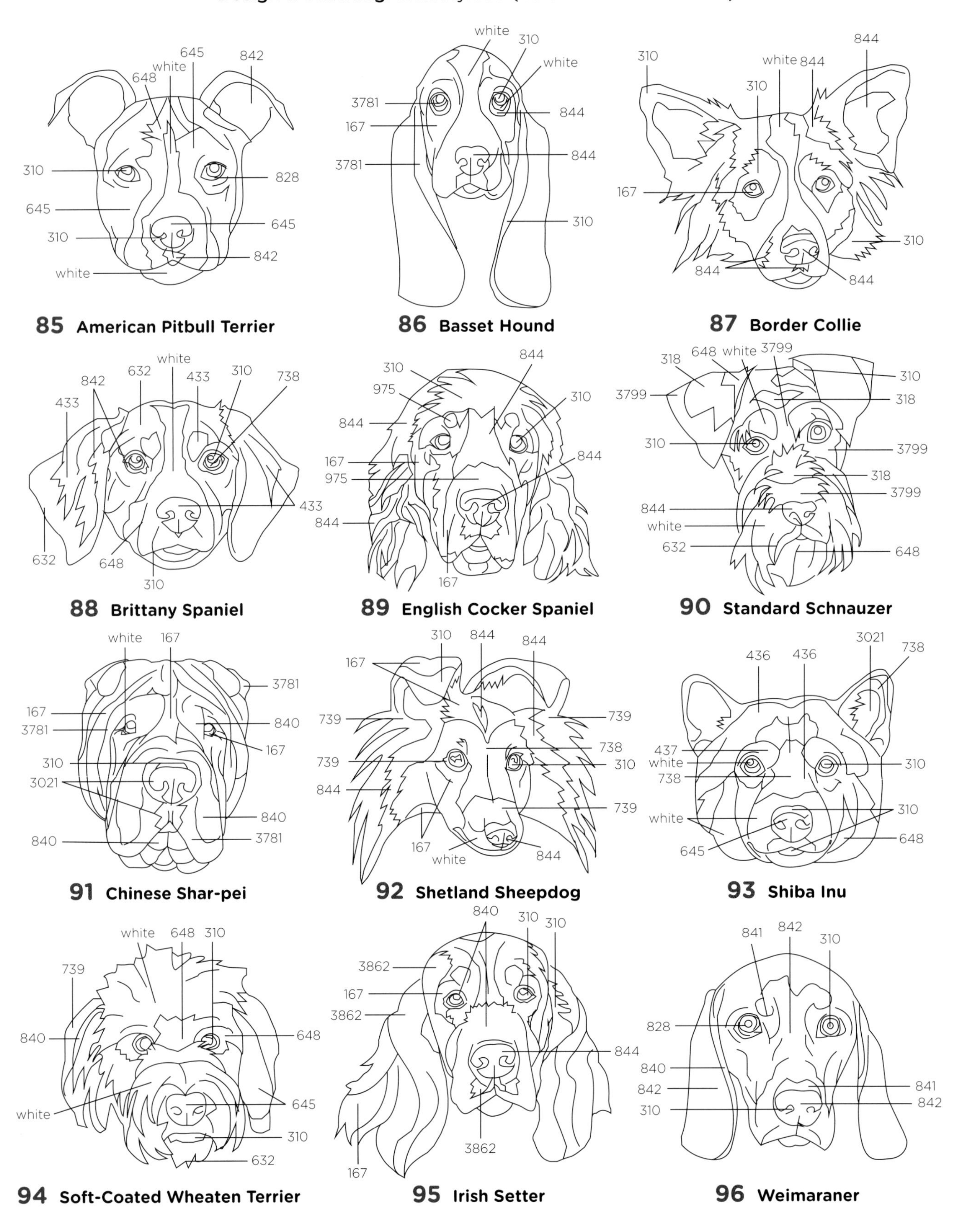

85 American Pitbull Terrier
86 Basset Hound
87 Border Collie
88 Brittany Spaniel
89 English Cocker Spaniel
90 Standard Schnauzer
91 Chinese Shar-pei
92 Shetland Sheepdog
93 Shiba Inu
94 Soft-Coated Wheaten Terrier
95 Irish Setter
96 Weimaraner

- Use 1 strand unless indicated with (#)
- # indicates color number
- Fill areas with Long and Short stitches unless otherwise indicated

85 American Pitbull Terrier

86 Basset Hound

87 Border Collie

88 Brittany Spaniel

89 English Cocker Spaniel

90 Standard Schnauzer

91 Chinese Shar-Pei

92 Shetland Sheepdog

93 Shiba Inu

94 Soft-Coated Wheaten Terrier

95 Irish Setter

96 Weimaraner

Just Call Me Spot

Motifs: Page 14
Design & Stitching: Chloe Redfern Embroidery (Chloe Redfern)

■ Use 1 strand except for fill areas which use 2 strands ■ # indicates color number ■ All outlines are stitched using back stitch with dark grey DMC 3799 ■ Dogs' eyes, noses and mouths are stitched using either one (for the smaller motifs) or two strands of black DMC 310 ■ The eyes and mouths are outlined in back stitch, and the nose and pupil are filled in using small straight stitches placed close together

Baby, I'm a Star!

Motifs: Page 15

Design & Stitching: Chloe Redfern Embroidery (Chloe Redfern)

- Use 1 strand except for fill areas which use 2 strands
- # indicates color number
- All outlines are stitched using back stitch with dark grey DMC 3799
- Dogs' eyes, noses and mouths are stitched using either one (for the smaller motifs) or 2 strands of black DMC 310
- The eyes and mouths are outlined in back stitch, and the nose and pupil are filled in using small straight stitches placed close together

Won't You Be My Friend?

Motifs: Page 16
Design & Stitching: Solipandi (Anja Lehmann)

- Use 1 strand unless indicated with (#)
- # indicates color number

Doggy Heaven

Motifs: Page 17

Design & Stitching: Solipandi (Anja Lehmann)

■ Use 1 strand unless indicated with (#) ■ # indicates color number

I Love My Job

Motifs: Page 18

Design & Stitching: MakikoArt (Oksana Kokovkina)

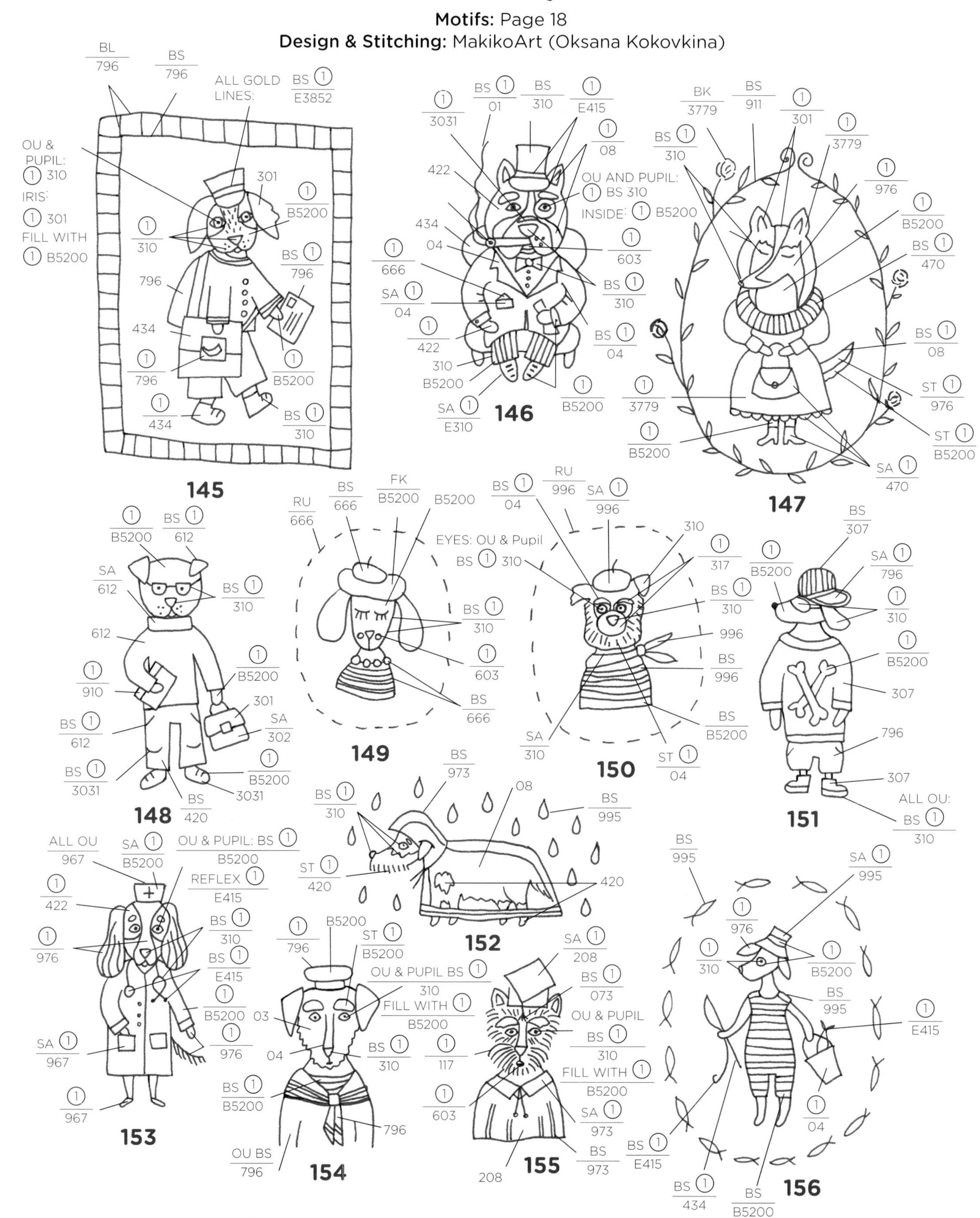

- Use 2 strands unless indicated with (#)
- # indicates color number
- Use outline stitch unless otherwise indicated

Sporty Pups

Motifs: Page 19
Design & Stitching: MakikoArt (Oksana Kokovkina)

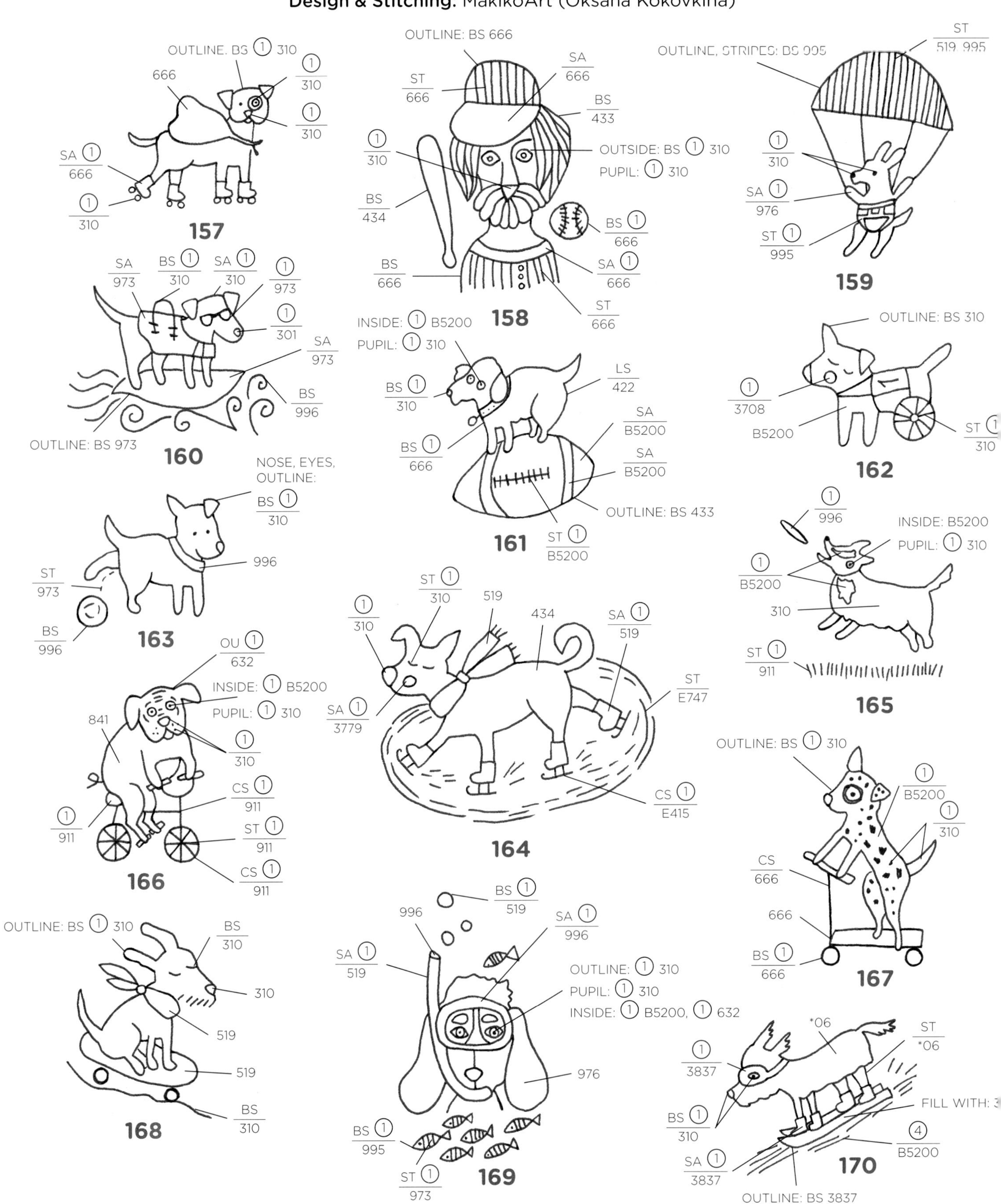

- Use 2 strands unless indicated with (#)
- # indicates color number
- Use outline stitch unless otherwise noted

Getting Into Stuff

Motifs: Page 20

Design & Stitching: MakikoArt (Oksana Kokovkina)

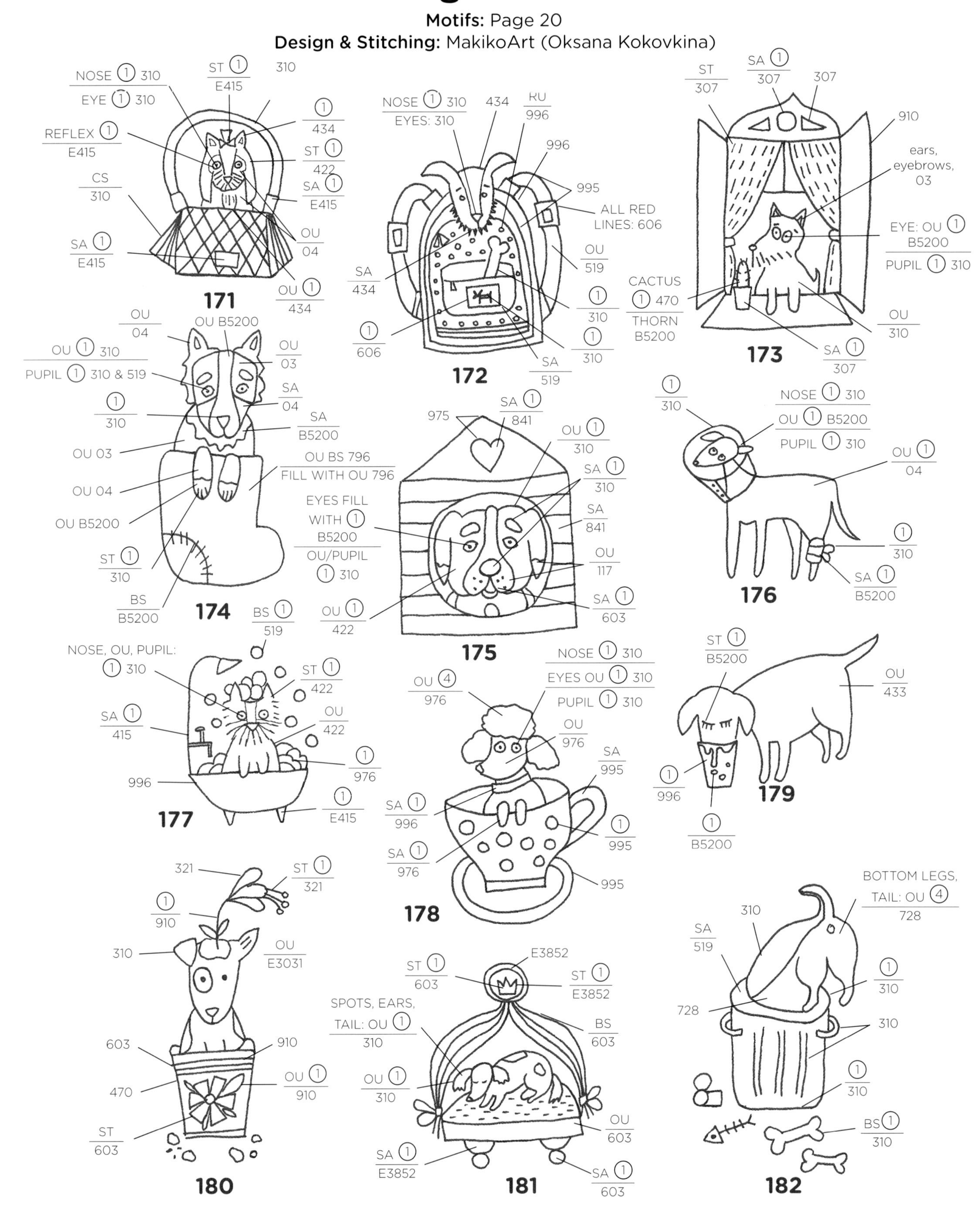

- Use 2 strands unless indicated with (#)
- Use back stitch unless otherwise noted
- # indicates color number

Getting Stuff Done

Motifs: Page 21
Design & Stitching: MakikoArt (Oksana Kokovkina)

183

ALL OU: BS 310
841
B5200
310
EYEBROWS, OU, PUPIL & NOSE: BS ① / 310
911
BS ① / 666
ST / 310

184

① / B5200
BS ① / 310
① / 839
B5200
OU & PUPIL: BS ① 310
IRIS: ① 435
INSIDE: B5200
EYE, OU, NOSE & EYEBROWS: BS ① / 435
OU: BS / 435
435
ST / 470

185

976
728
OU BS / 976
BS ① / 310
① / 310
① / 976
BS ① / 603

186

310
B5200
3779
EYE, OU & PUPILS: BS ① 310
INSIDE: ① 519
① / 310
SA / 947
947
BS ① / 603

187

EYES: OU & PUPIL BS ① 310
INSIDE ① B5200
ST / 04
BS / 911
① / B5200
BS ① / 310
04
BS / 66
B5200

188

EYE, OU & PUPILS: BS ① 310
INSIDE: ① 519
B5200
① / 310
BS ① / 603
BS ① / 603
① / 310
① / 434

189

OU BS ① / 04
① / 04
EYE OU ① B5200
PUPIL ① 310
310
ST / 04
ST / 04
① / 310
① / B5200

190

ST / 04
310
BS / 04
① / 470
EYES: OU & PUPIL BS ① / 310
BS / 04
BS ① / E310
BS ① / E415

191

BS ① / 310
3779
310
117
BS ① / 310
B5200
310
3779

192

BS ① / 995
975
301
① / 310
976
3779
839
BS ① / 519
B5200
① / 301
975

193

BS ① / 976
975
BS ① / 605
① / 310
976
976
EYE: OU ① B5200
PUPIL ① 310

194

ST / 976
BS ① / 310
911
BS ① / B5200
ST / 728
310
BS ① / 310
ST ① / 470
728
① / 301
BS / 911
BS / B5200
① / 422

- Use 2 strands unless indicated with (#)
- # indicates color number
- Use outline stitch unless otherwise noted

Dog Days

Motifs: Page 22

Design & Stitching: MakikoArt (Oksana Kokovkina)

■ Use 1 strand unless indicated with (#) ■ Use 1 strand and back stitch, color 310, for nose, eyes, and smooth/straight parts ■ Use 1 strand straight stitch, color 310, for fur, tail, and beard ■ # indicates color number

Scruffy Chic

Motifs: Page 23

Design & Stitching: MakikoArt (Oksana Kokovkina)

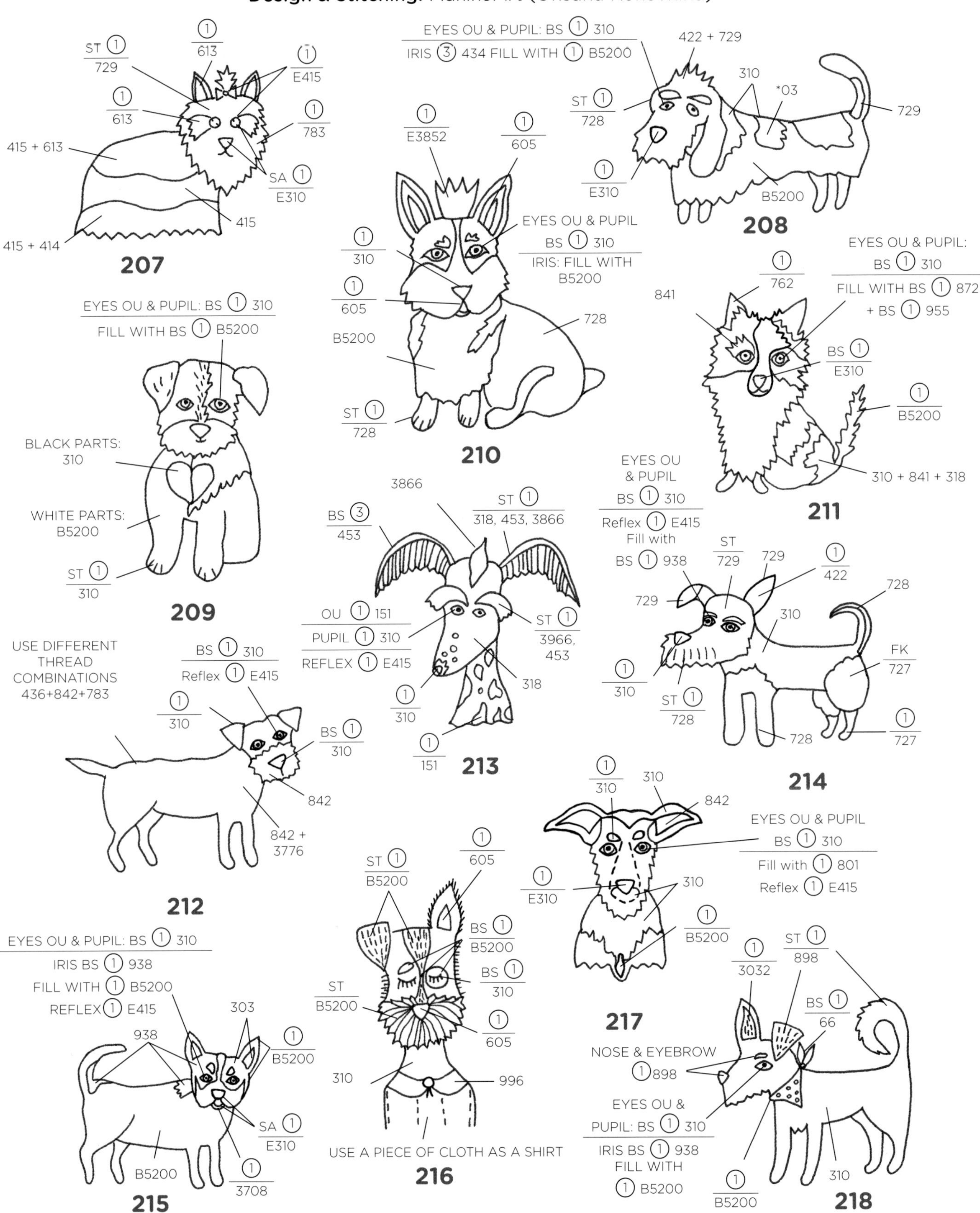

- Use 2 strands unless indicated with (#)
- # indicates color number
- Use outline stitch unless otherwise indicated

Dazzling Dogs

Motifs: Page 24
Design & Stitching: MakikoArt (Oksana Kokovkina)

- Use 2 strands unless indicated with (#)
- Use back stitch unless otherwise noted
- # indicates color number

Interspecies Love

Motifs: Page 25
Design & Stitching: MakikoArt (Oksana Kokovkina)

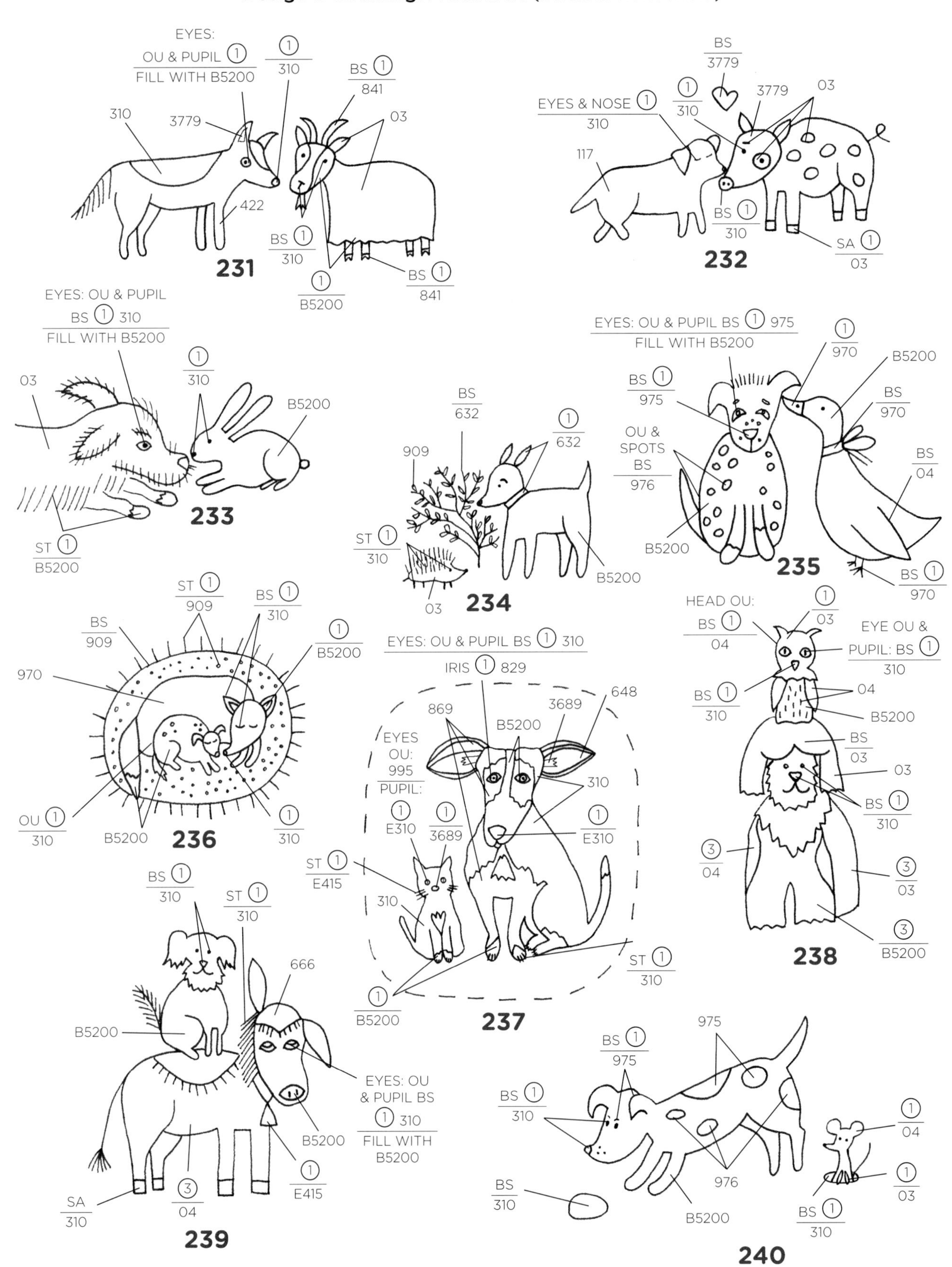

- Use 2 strands unless indicated with (#)
- # indicates color number
- Use outline stitch unless otherwise noted

Seasons & Celebrations

Motifs: Page 26

Design & Sttitching: MakikoArt (Oksana Kokovkina)

241

OU: BS 3779 · B5200 · ST 3779 · SA 976 · OU: BS 435 · 435 · E415 · (1) 310 · 310 · SA 976 · B5200

242

BS 470 · SA 728 · EYES: B5200 · PUPIL: 310 · 967 · BS (1) 310 · B5200 · 3708 · SA 973 · 728 · OU: BS 435

243

SA (1) E967 · (1) 310 · OU: BS 3779 · B5200 · (1) 422 · (1) B310 · PUPIL & OU BS (1) 310 · 3708 · (1) 310 · B5200 · 3779 · BS 5200 · 310 · ST (1) 310 · 422

244

OU: BS (1) 310 · INSIDE (1) B5200 · PUPIL (1) 310 · BS (1) 519 · SA (1) E334 · 976 · B520 · 433 · 976 · PETALS: ST (1) 519 · MIDDLE: SA (1) E334 · ST (1) 470

245

BS E3852 · ST E3852 · ST (1) E3852 · BS (1) E3852 · PUPIL 310 · ST (1) B5200 · (1) 321 · 310 · E3852 · (1) 742

246

(1) 742 · BS 310 · BS 310 · 742 · 310 · ST (1) 310 · 310

247

ST 307 · 797 · 307 · (1) B5200 · PUPIL (1) 310 · ST (1) 310 · 434 · 307 · (4) 434 · ST (1) 09 · 422

248

BS 310 · (1) 307 · BS (1) 310 · BS 422 · BS (1) 310 · 307 · BS 310 · (1) 310 · ST (1) 422

249

ST 307 · 3837 · SA 307 · 420 · 422 · SA 3837 · 310 · SA 3837

250

BS 33 · 3812 · (1) 310 · 33 · BS (1) 310

251

420 · OU: BS (1) 310 · PUPIL 310 · INSIDE (1) B5200 · (1) 3708 · BS (1) 310 · 975 · 310 · B5200 · (1) 3708 · OU: BS 420 · SA 970

252

OU: BS 310 · ST 310 · ST B5200 · 07 · 07 · 310 · B5200 · 310 · GLASSES BS 310 · INSIDE B5200 · PUPIL 310 · ST (1) 07 · 973 · 608 · 3799 · ST (1) 07 · 07

- Use 2 strands unless indicated with (#)
- # indicates color number
- Use outline stitch unless otherwise indicated

Seasons & Celebrations

Motifs: Page 27

Design & Stitching: MakikoArt (Oksana Kokovkina)

- Use 2 strands unless indicated with (#)
- # indicates color number
- Use satin stitch unless otherwise indicated

Astrodogical Signs (without dogs)

Motifs: Page 28
Design & Stitching: How Could You? Clothing (Mia Alexi)

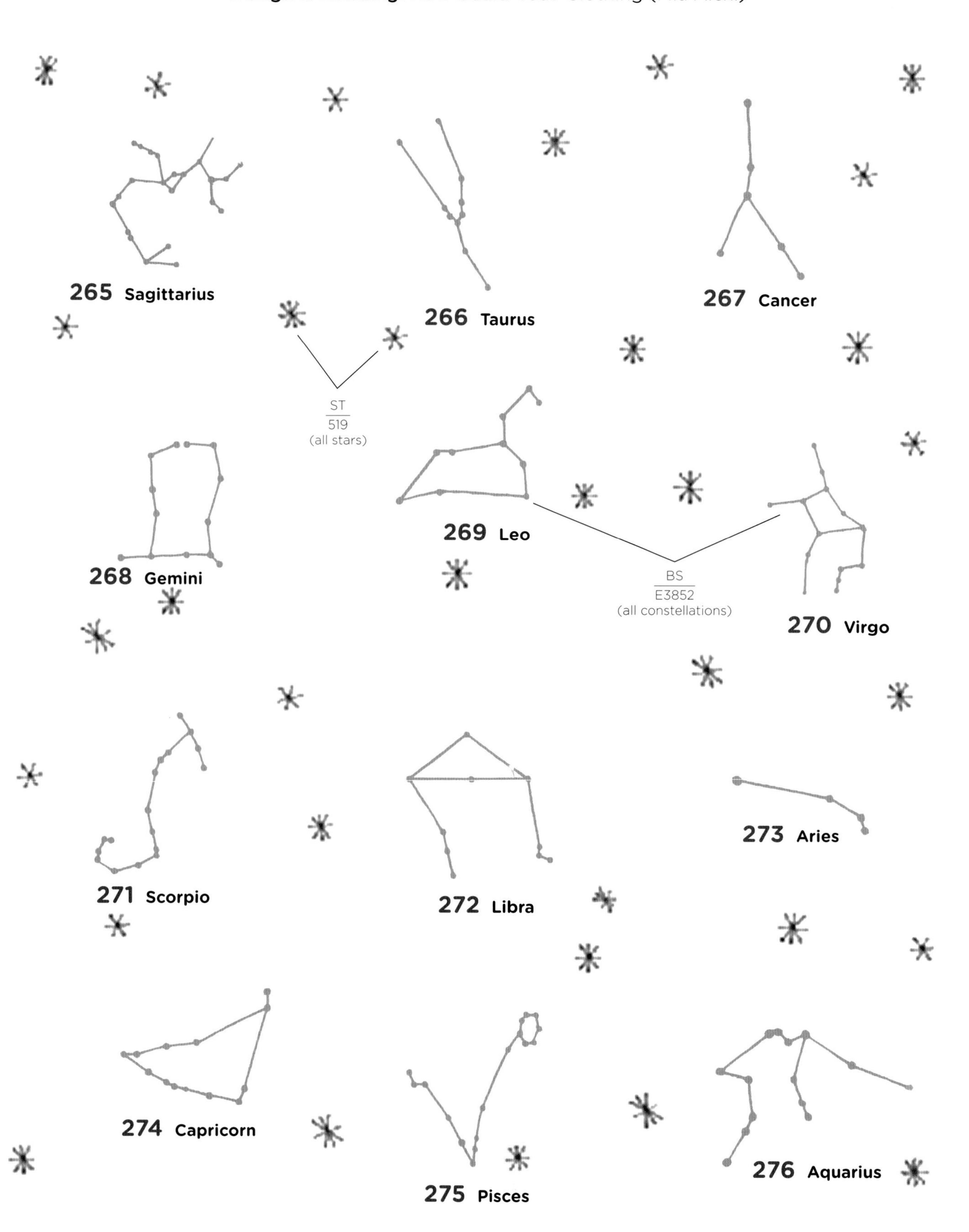

■ Use 2 strands unless indicated with (#) ■ Gold constellations use DMC E3852 Dark Gold (metallic floss) ■ Blue stars use DMC 519 Sky Blue ■ Use backstitch for constellation lines ■ Use French knots for gold constellation stars ■ For the blue stars use a straight stitch

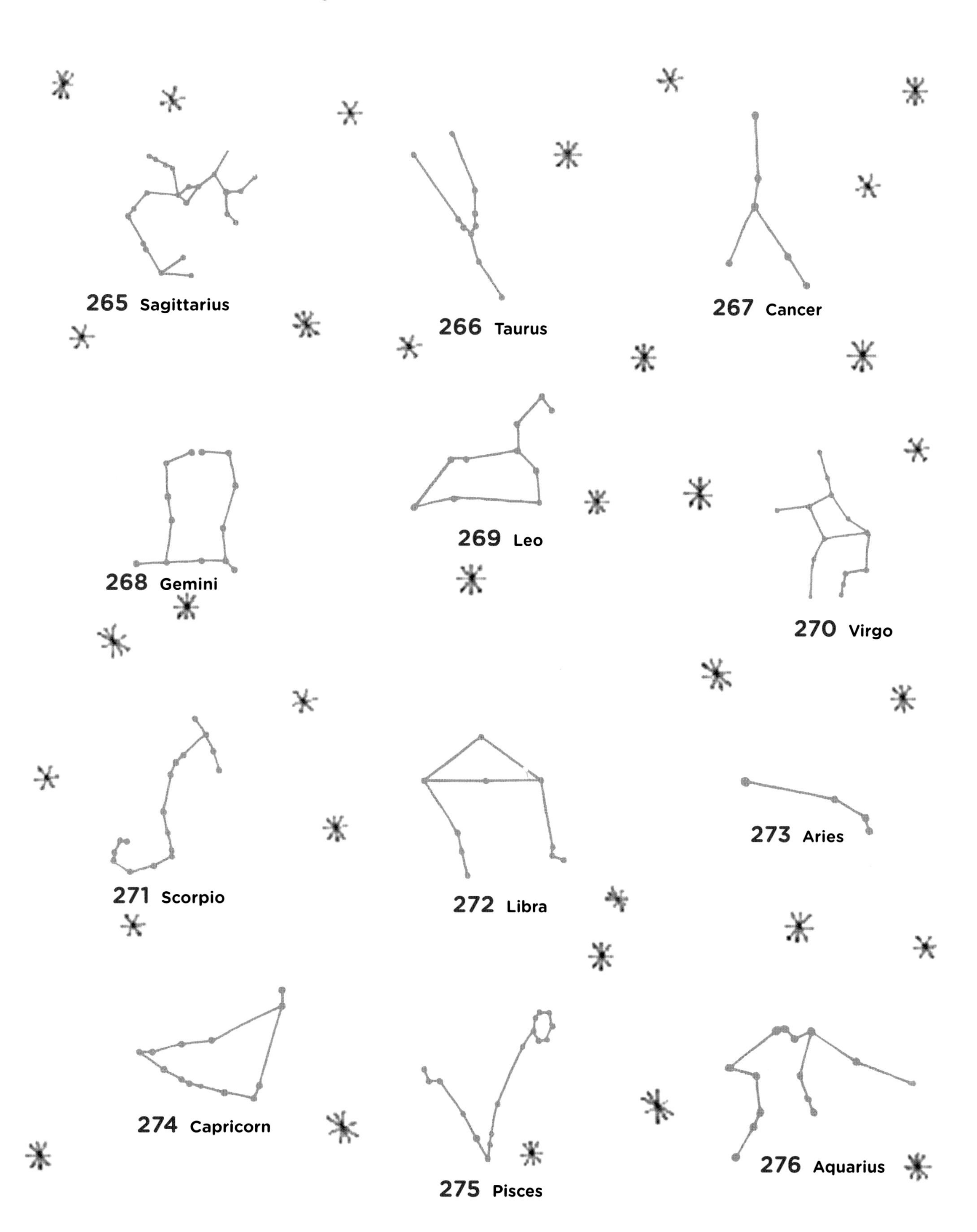

Astrodogical Signs (with dogs)

Motifs: Page 29

Design & Stitching: How Could You? Clothing (Mia Alexi)

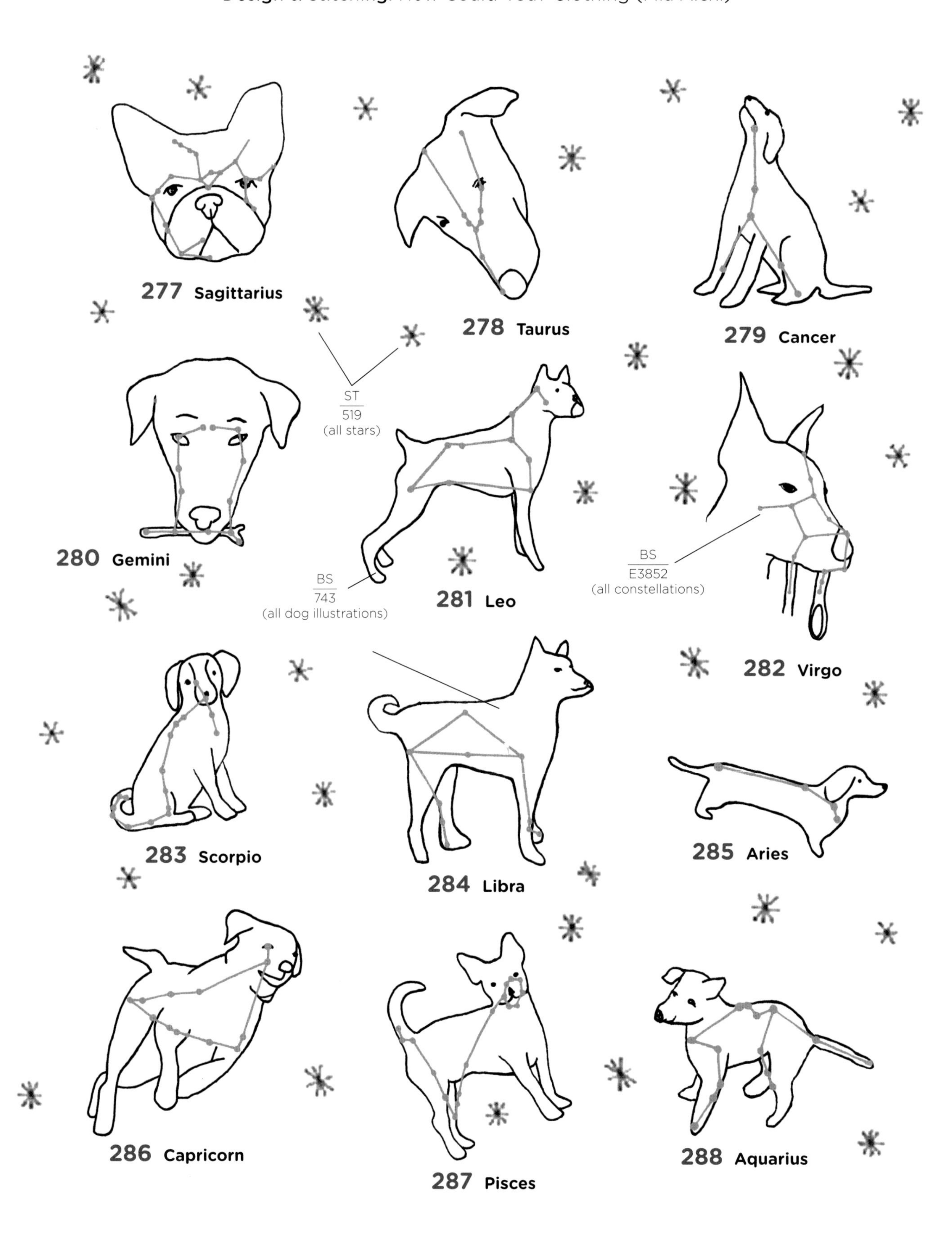

■ Use 2 strand unless indicated with (#) ■ For yellow dog outline use DMC 743 Med. Yellow ■ For gold constellations use DMC E3852 Dark Gold (metallic floss) ■ For blue stars use DMC 519 Sky Blue ■ Use backstitch for dog outlines and constellation lines ■ Use French knots for gold constellation stars ■ For blue stars use a straight stitch

Alpha Dogs

Motifs: Page 30
Design & Stitching: How Could You? Clothing (Mia Alexi)

■ Use 2 strands unless indicated with (#) ■ For alphabet use DMC 519 Sky Blue ■ For dogs a & i use DMC 435 Very Light Brown ■ For dogs b, g & m use DMC 898 Very Dark Coffee Brown ■ For dogs c & e use DMC 744 Pale Yellow ■ For dogs d & j use DMC 310 Black ■ For dogs f & k use DMC 976 Med. Golden Brown ■ For dogs h & l use DMC 644 Med. Beige Gray ■ Use satin stitch for the letters ■ Use backstitch for the dogs

Alpha Dogs

Motifs: Page 31

Design & Stitching: How Could You? Clothing (Mia Alexi)

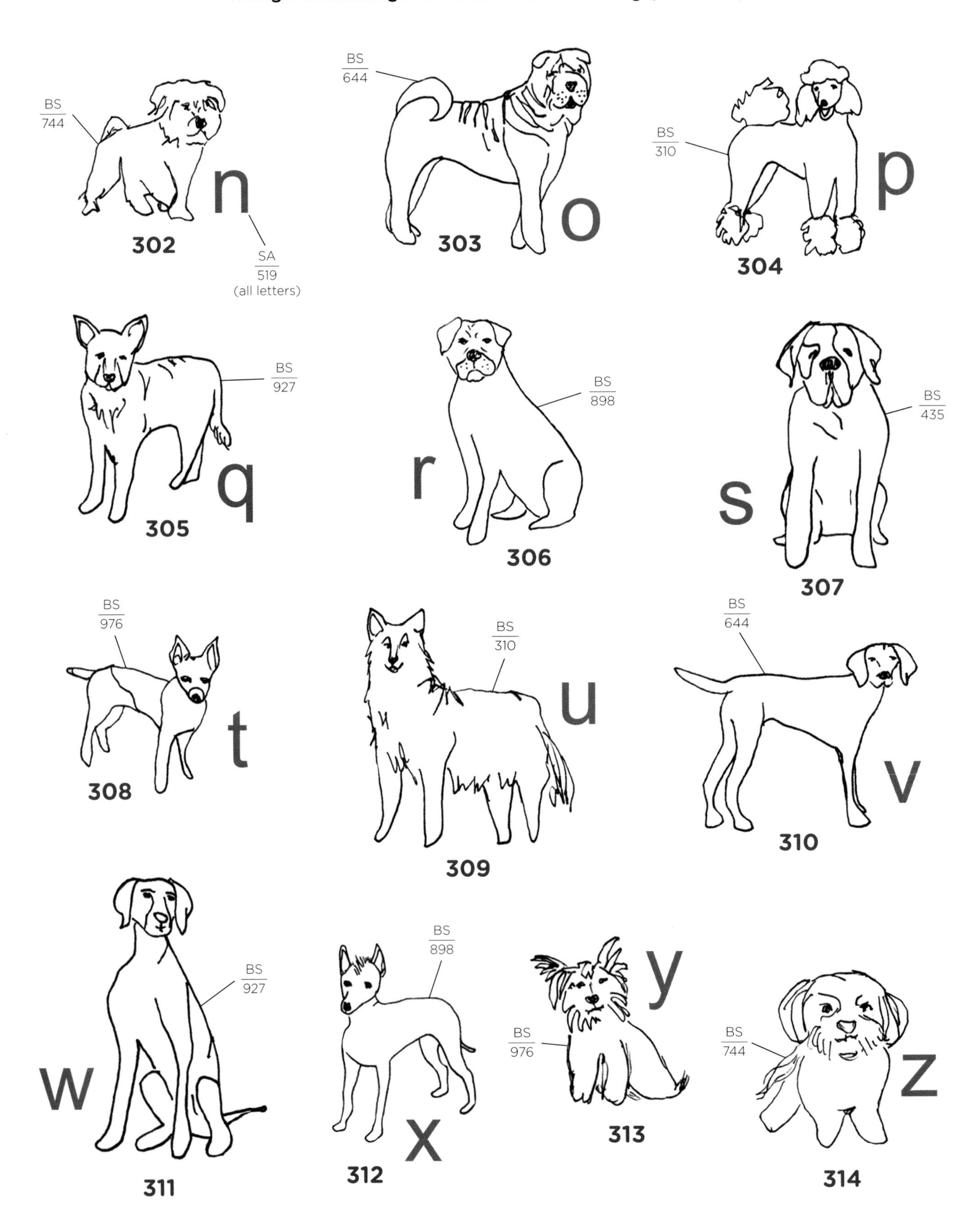

■ Use 2 strands unless indicated with (#) ■ For the alphabet use DMC 519 Sky Blue ■ For dog s use DMC 435 Very Light Brown ■ For dogs r & x use DMC 898 Very Dark Coffee Brown ■ For dogs n & z use DMC 744 Pale Yellow ■ For dogs p & u use DMC 310 Black ■ For dogs t & y use DMC 976 Med. Golden Brown ■ For dogs o & v use DMC 644 Med. Beige Gray ■ For dogs q and w use DMC 927 Light Gray Green ■ Use satin stitch for letters ■ Use Backstitch for dogs

Look-Alikes: Pups & Their Peeps

Motifs: Page 32
Design & Stitching: Stitch People (Elizabeth Dabczynski)

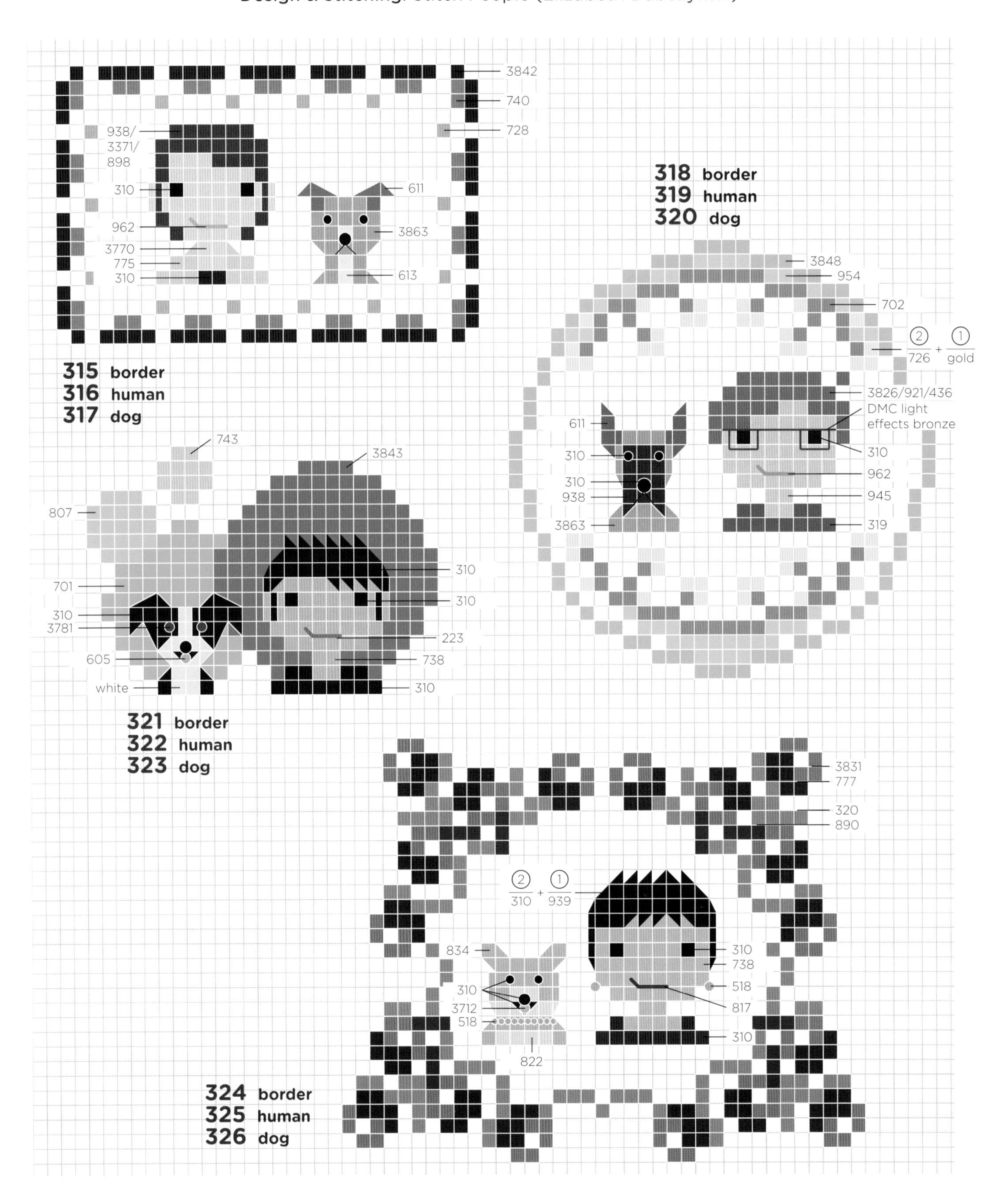

■ Use 3 strands unless indicated with (#) ■ # indicates color number ■ Use cross stitch unless otherwise indicated ■ For dog's eyes and round noses use French knots ■ For lines like people's mouths, use a straight stitch

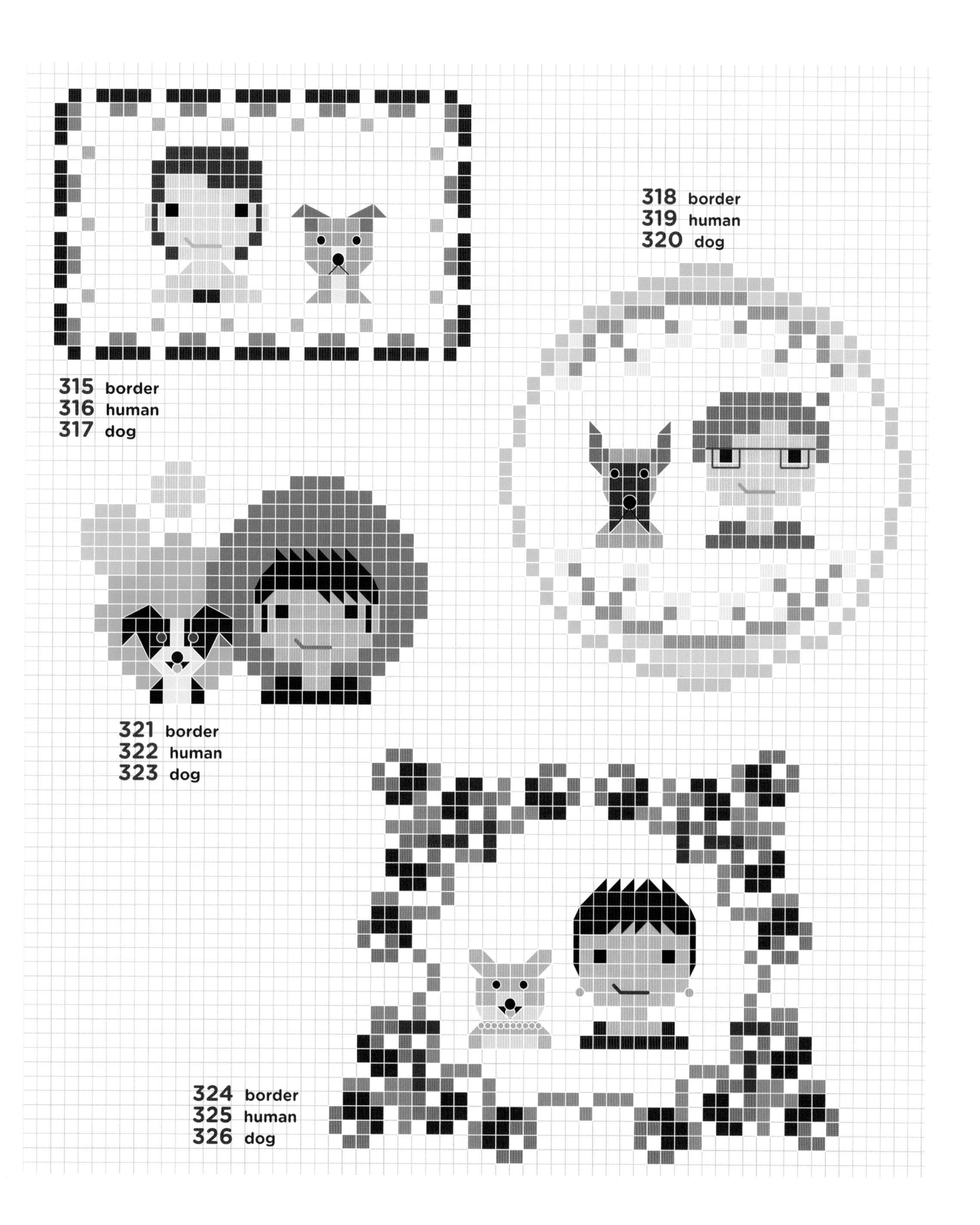

Look-Alikes: Pups & Their Peeps

Motifs: Page 33
Design & Stitching: Stitch People (Elizabeth Dabczynski)

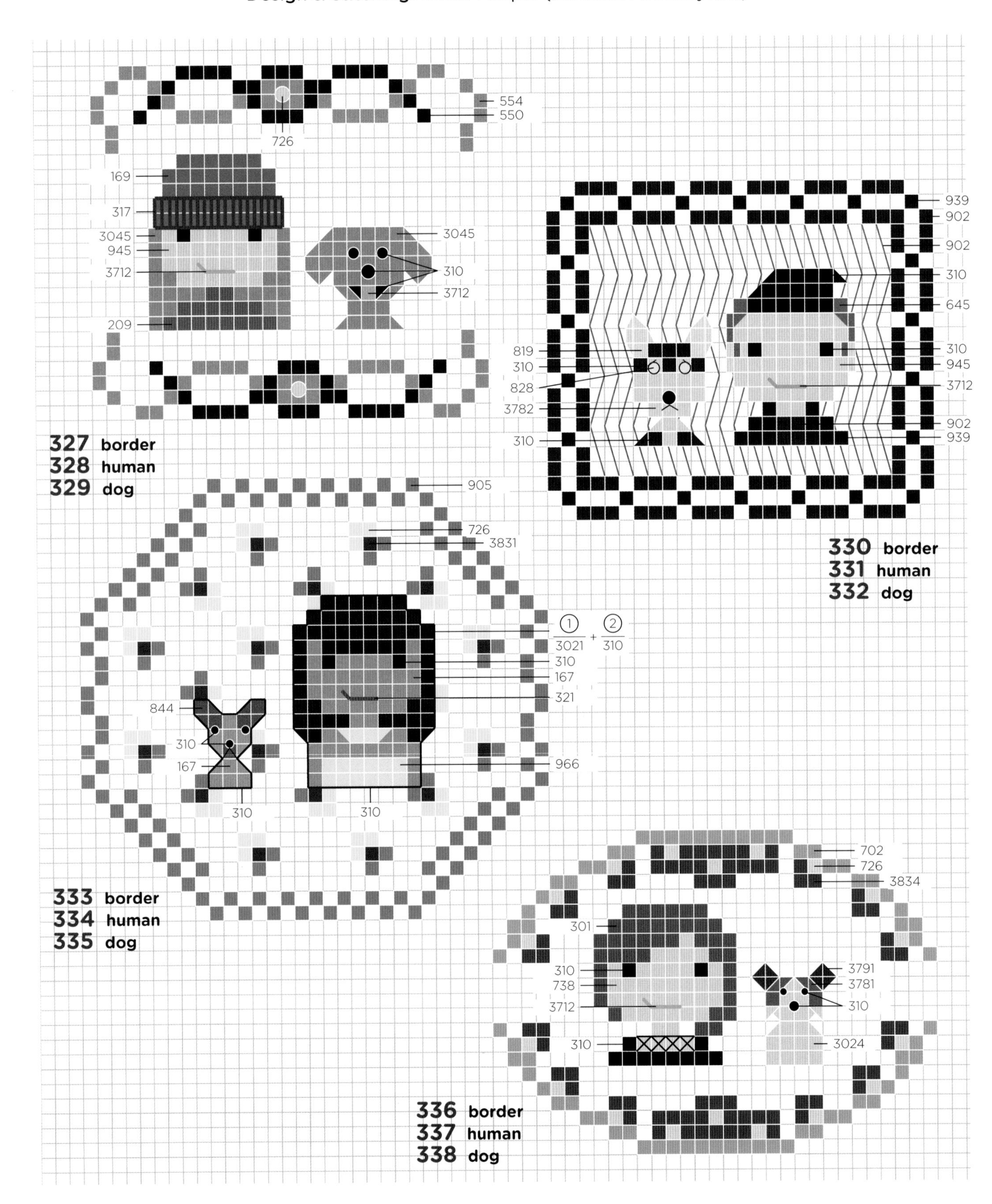

■ Use 3 strands unless indicated with (#) ■ # indicates color number ■ Use cross stitch unless otherwise indicated ■ For dog's eyes and round noses use French knots ■ For lines like people's mouths, use a straight stitch

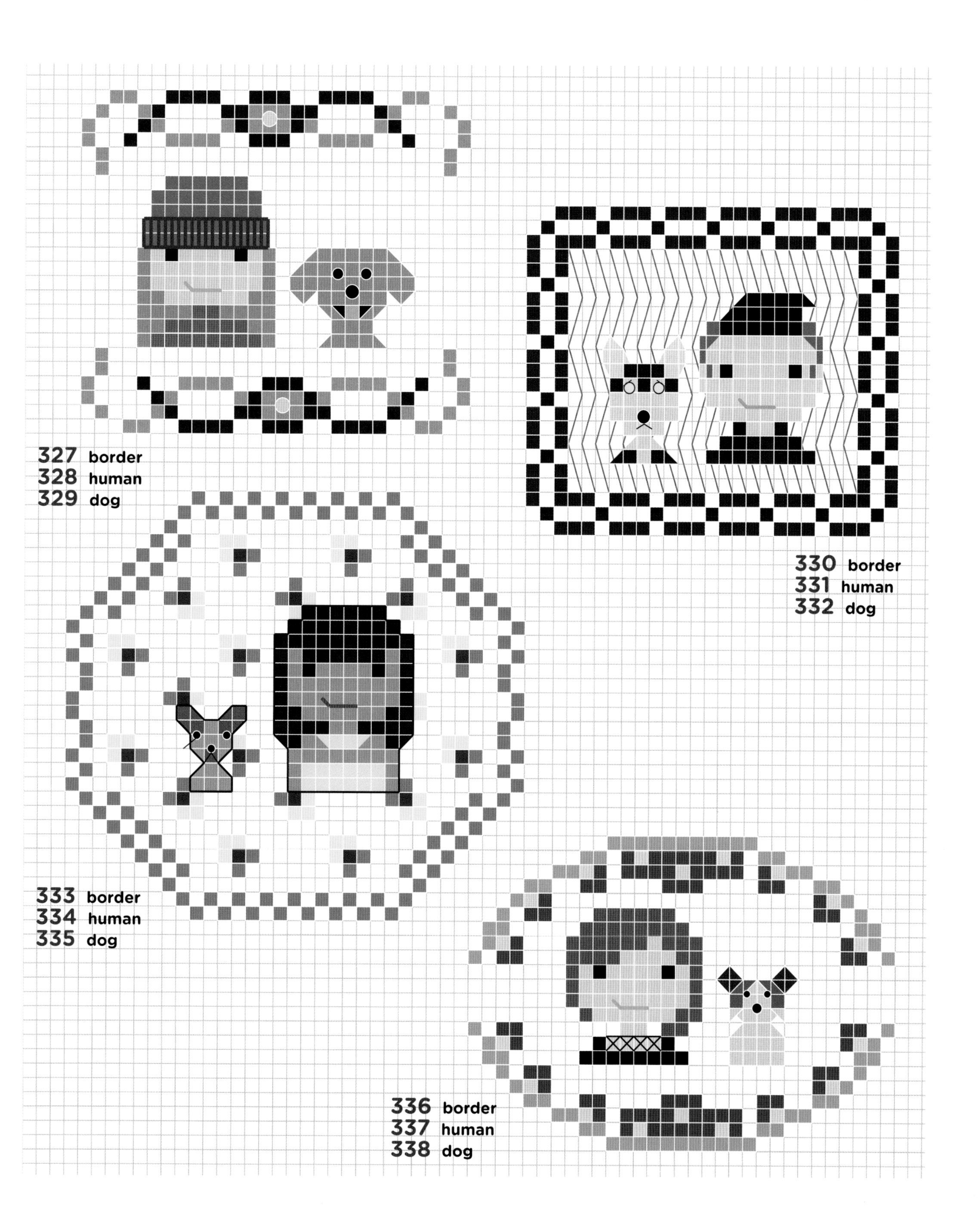

Look-Alikes: Pups & Their Peeps

Motifs: Page 34
Design & Stitching: Stitch People (Elizabeth Dabczynski)

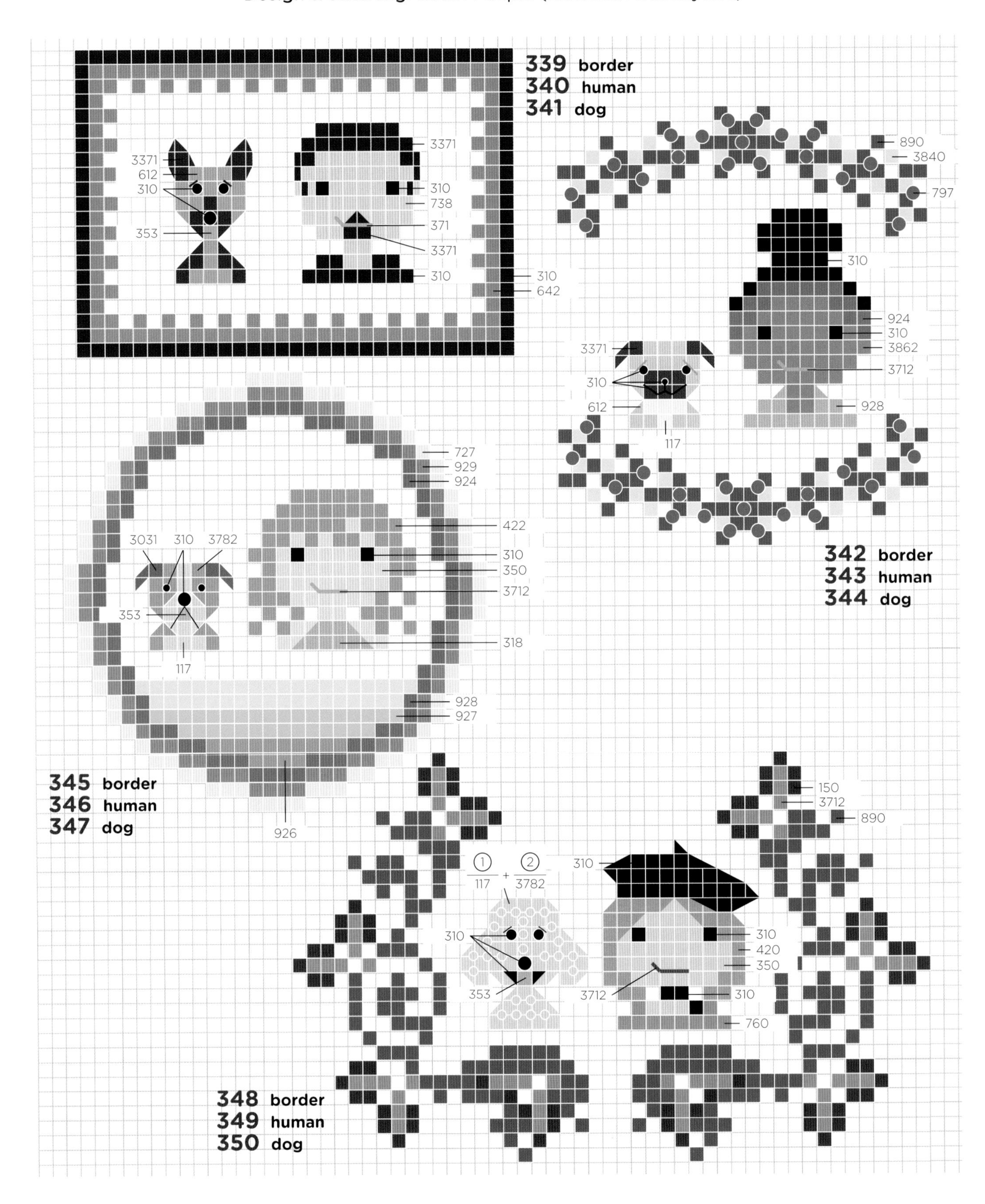

■ Use 3 strands unless indicated with (#) ■ # indicates color number ■ Use cross stitch unless otherwise indicated ■ For dog's eyes and round noses use French knots ■ For lines like people's mouths, use a straight stitch

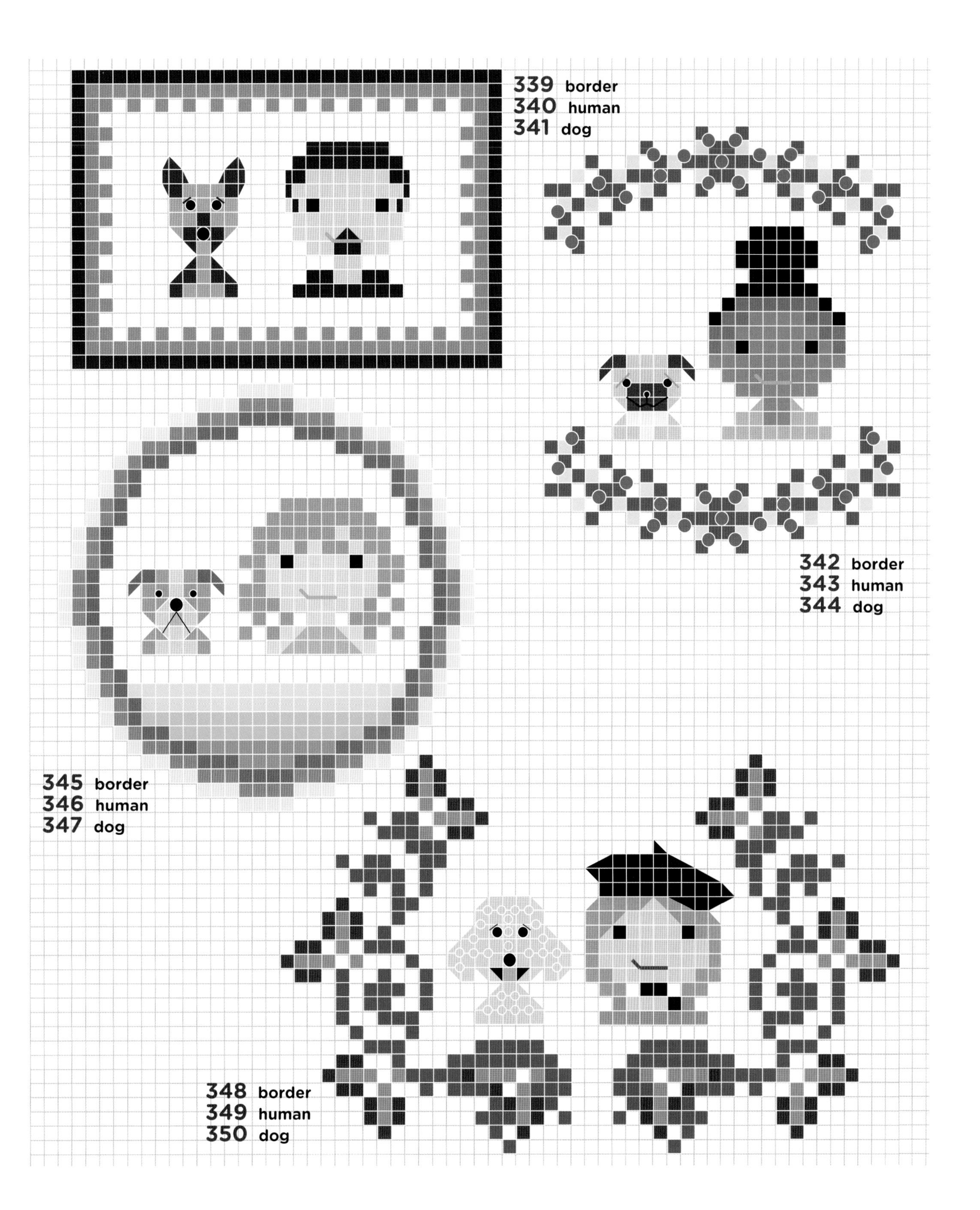

Look-Alikes: Pups & Their Peeps

Motifs: Page 35
Design & Stitching: Stitch People (Elizabeth Dabczynski)

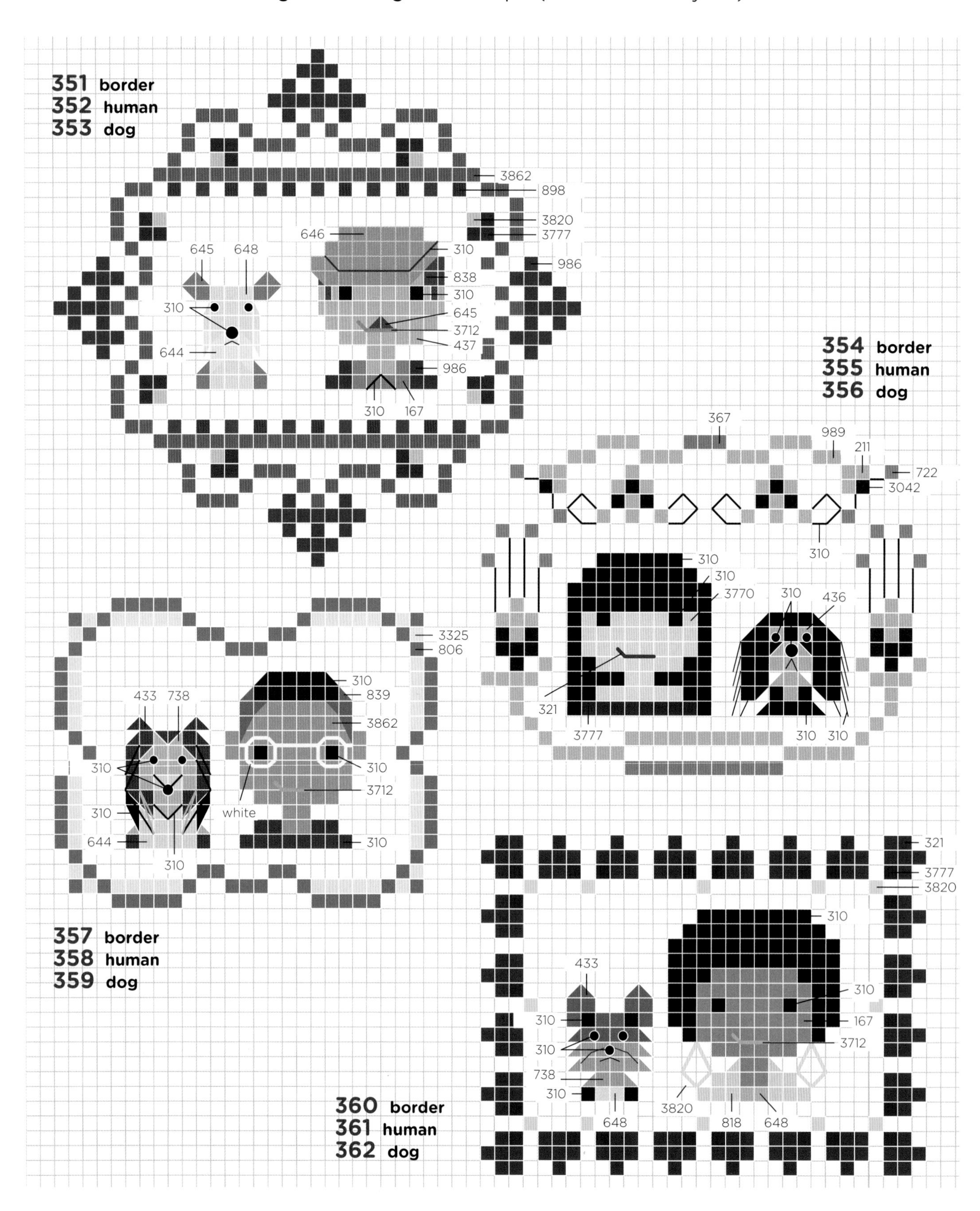

■ Use 3 strands unless indicated with (#) ■ # indicates color number ■ Use cross stitch unless otherwise indicated ■ For dog's eyes and round noses use French knots ■ For lines like people's mouths, use a straight stitch

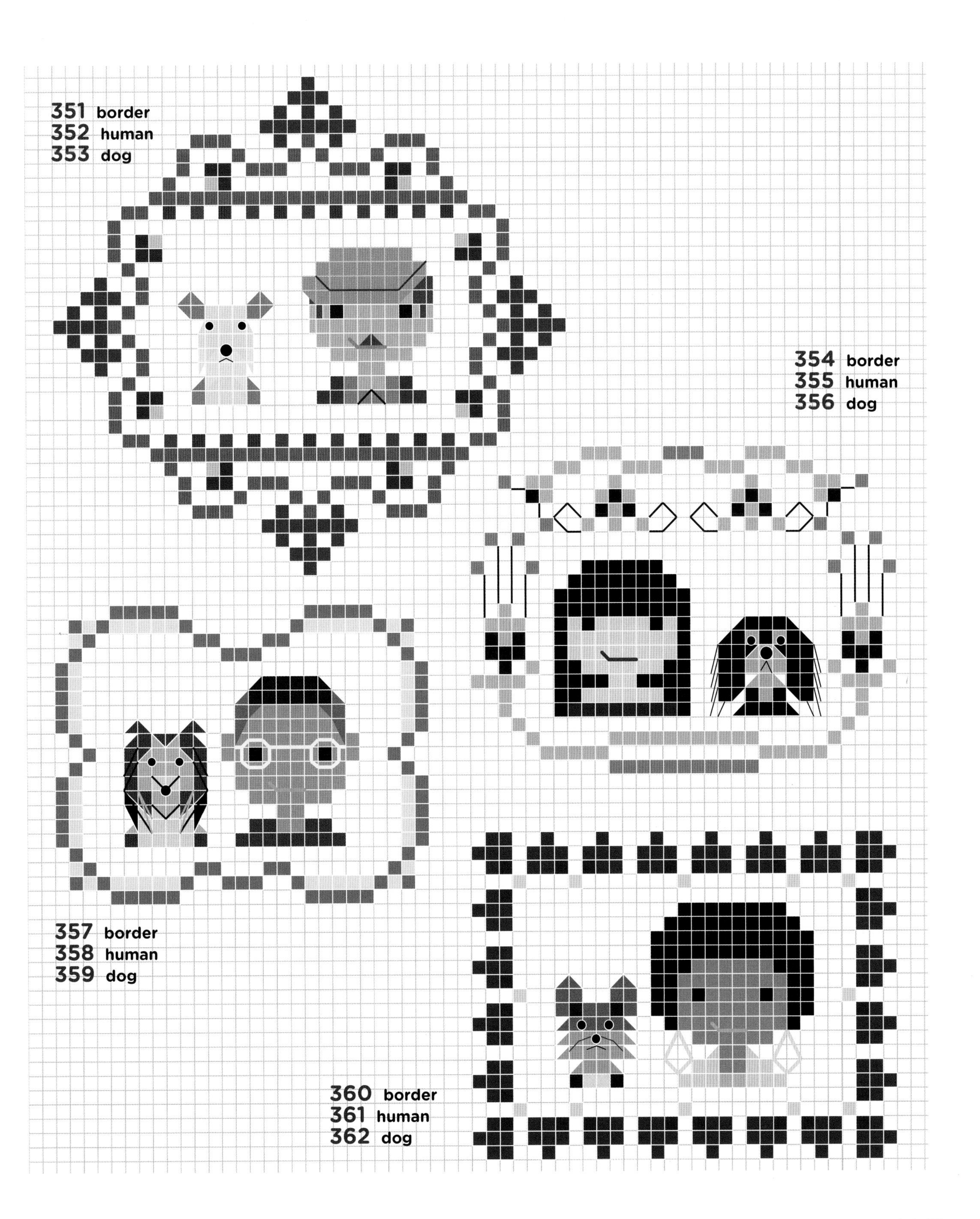

Me Time

Motifs: Page 36
Design & Stitching: Miho Starling—mipomipo handmade

- Use 1 strand unless indicated with (#)
- # indicates color number

363 364 365 366 367 368 369 370 371 372 373 374

Doga Poses

Motifs: Page 37

Design & Stitching: Miho Starling—mipomipo handmade

- Use 1 strand unless indicated with (#)
- # indicates color number

  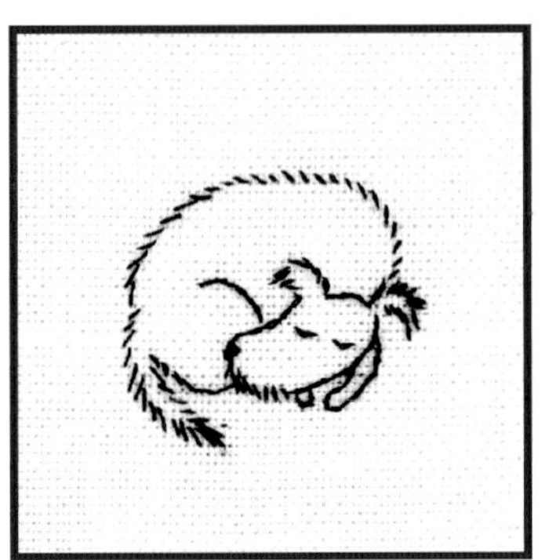 

Brimming with creative inspiration, how-to projects, and useful information to enrich your everyday life, Quarto Knows is a favorite destination for those pursuing their interests and passions. Visit our site and dig deeper with our books into your área of interest: Quarto Creates, Quarto Cooks, Quarto Homes, Quarto Lives, Quarto Drives, Quarto Explores, Quarto Gifts, or Quarto Kids.

First Published in 2019 by Quarry Books, an imprint of The Quarto Group,
100 Cummings Center, Suite 265-D, Beverly, MA 01915, USA.
T (978) 282-9590 F (978) 283-2742 QuartoKnows.com

Quarry Books titles are also available at discount for retail, wholesale, promotional, and bulk purchase. For details, contact the Special Sales Manager by email at specialsales@quarto.com or by mail at The Quarto Group, Attn: Special Sales Manager, 100 Cummings Center, Suite 265-D, Beverly, MA, 01915.

10 9 8 7 6 5 4 3 2 1

ISBN: 978-1-63159-613-1

Digital edition published in 2019

Library of Congress Cataloging-in-Publication Data available

Cover Image: MakikoArt (Oksana Kokovkina)
Page Layout: Megan Jones Design
Photography and Illustrations: MakikoArt / Oksana Kokovkina (pages 18–27, 38–55); Insanitynice / Valentina Castillo Mora (6–13); Chloe Redfern Embroidery / Chloe Redfern (14, 15); Solipandi / Anja Lehmann (16, 17); How Could You? Clothing / Mia Alexi (28–31); Stitch People / Elizabeth Dabczynski (32–35); Miho Starling / mipomipo handmade (36, 37).

Printed in China